SKILLS FOR BUSINESS ENGLISH

Student Book 1

David Kerridge

DELTA
PUBLISHING

Map of the book

UNIT	FUNCTIONS	SKILLS AND LANGUAGE FOCUS
1 First contacts	Making business contacts Arranging a meeting Greetings and introductions Talking about jobs	A Reading and writing • company job titles; an introductory letter; correcting notes and writing a reply B Listening • greetings and introductions; company descriptions and activities C Speaking • greetings expressions; job descriptions Role plays: talking about work and interests
2 Travelling for business	Travel language Making reservations Organising trips Making enquiries	A Reading and writing • enquiries and responses; a letter outlining a project; an e-mail with fax reply B Listening • airport announcements; greetings; checking into a hotel C Speaking • flight information Role plays: arranging travel and accommodation
3 Exchanging information	Making telephone calls Leaving messages Asking about products and services	A Reading and writing • telephone expressions; an introductory letter; a reply from notes B Listening • telephone conversations: outline of a company's services; hotel reservations C Speaking • basic telephone expressions Role plays: making arrangements and leaving messages
4 Meetings and opinions	Taking part in meetings Asking for and giving opinions Agreeing and disagreeing	A Reading and writing • meetings expressions; an introductory letter; a reply from notes B Listening • expressions of agreement and opinion; making decisions C Speaking • ideas, opinions and responses Role plays: expressing opinions, agreement and disagreement
5 Instructions and warnings	Giving instructions Understanding regulations Describing processes Suggesting alternatives	A Reading and writing • notices and instructions; a letter about a business trip; a fax from notes; written directions B Listening • finding locations on a map; safety notices; process descriptions C Speaking • possibilities and requests Role plays: making requests and responding; describing locations and following descriptions
6 Trends and predictions	Analysing trends Describing patterns Making predictions	A Reading and writing • language of trends; banking functions; economic and demographic information; a short report B Listening • a presentation about economic trends; post-presentation questions; information from graphs C Speaking • graph descriptions Role plays: working with graphs and demographic information

UNIT	FUNCTIONS	SKILLS AND LANGUAGE FOCUS
7 Company profiles	Describing companies Explaining choices Justifying decisions	A **Reading and writing** • graphs and descriptions; a company profile; an application form B **Listening** • telephone calls: dealing with problems, choices and solutions C **Speaking** • verbs relating to company performance; a company history Role plays: company presentations
8 Suggestions and reasons	Making suggestions Suggesting alternatives Justifying decisions Giving reasons	A **Reading and writing** • a letter containing suggestions; responding to the letter with alternative suggestions and reasons B **Listening** • a meeting to negotiate a contract; a telephone conversation focusing on persuasion C **Speaking** • making suggestions and giving reasons Role plays: negotiating
9 Terms of sale and delivery	Negotiating terms of sale Agreeing delivery dates Making decisions	A **Reading and writing** • terms of sale questions and responses; information transfer using a price list; completing an e-mail B **Listening** • preparing a negotiating position; extract from a negotiation C **Speaking** • prepositions of numbers and time; matching offers and responses Role plays: negotiating on the telephone
10 Technical and social exchanges	Exchanging technical information Quantities and dimensions Making invitations Social conversation	A **Reading and writing** • describing dimensions; technical specifications; a formal letter of acceptance B **Listening** • a technical presentation; socialising in a restaurant C **Speaking** • suitable subjects for social conversation; making invitations and responding Role plays: social situations
11 Enquiries and complaints	Making enquiries Answering enquiries Dealing with complaints	A **Reading and writing** • polite questions; a conference programme; correcting an e-mail enquiry B **Listening** • enquiries and complaints at a conference C **Speaking** • practising enquiries and responses Role plays: making and dealing with enquiries, requests and complaints
12 Tasks and teams	Setting tasks Organising teams Defining responsibilities Working to deadlines	A **Reading and writing** • describing responsibilities; a newspaper interview; tasks and deadlines from a flow-chart; completing a fax B **Listening** • confirming arrangements and dealing with problems; planning ahead C **Speaking** • management responsibility, deadlines and objectives Role plays: negotiating responsibilities and company reorganisation

First contacts

- making business contacts
- arranging a meeting
- greetings and introductions
- talking about jobs

BEFORE YOU START

1 In the column on the left (1–5) are examples of the main skills in this unit. Match them with the expressions in the column on the right (A–E). The first has been done as an example.

1 Arranging a meeting — A I'd like you to meet Carla.
2 Introducing yourself — B We manufacture boats.
3 Introducing colleagues — C May I suggest Friday at 9 am?
4 Offering — D Good afternoon, my name's Jim.
5 Talking about companies — E Would you like a drink?

2 The following words may be new. Check that you understand them.
LAWYER – a legal expert (noun: LAW, adjective: LEGAL)
FIBREGLASS RESINS – materials used to manufacture pleasure boats
HULL – the "body" of a boat
DECK – the "floor" of a boat

A Reading and writing

In this unit (as well as in Units 5 and 9) we will look at two companies.

POLYCARACAS A Venezuelan company. It is located in Caracas and employs 230 people. It manufactures fibreglass resins used to make the hulls and decks of sailing boats.
Managing Director – Manuel Ortega
Production Manager – Juanita Castro
Export Manager – Carla Naranjo
Receptionist – Marisol Fuentes
Assistant – Hugo Mendez

Florida MARINE An American company which makes boats. It is based in Miami and has 250 employees.
Chief Executive Officer – Jim Prior
Purchasing Manager – Michelle Henderson
Finance Manager – Jack Ramsey

1 Look at the information about Polycaracas. Complete the following sentences. The first has been done as an example.

1 Manuel Ortega is the *Managing Director*.
He is the head of the company.

2 _____ _____ works in the Production Department.

3 _____ _____ is responsible for foreign sales, and reports directly to the Managing Director.

4 Hugo Mendez is the _____ and doesn't travel much.

5 _____ _____'s main responsibilities are welcoming visitors and answering telephone calls.

Mark these statements T (for True) or F (for False). Correct the sentences you think are false.

1 The Vietnamese government wants to modernise its road
   transport.   T   F
2 Road transport is efficient between Hanoi and Hong Gai.   T   F
3 Hong Gai may lose business in the future if communications
   are not improved.   T   F
4 The Vietnamese government wants a loan of $100 million from
   foreign sources.   T   F
5 Eighty per cent of the sum will come from the Asian Investment
   Bank.   T   F
6 Two Vietnamese will visit France to discuss the project.   T   F

2 Martin Reynolds wrote a formal reply to the letter, saying that his bank was interested in the project and had arranged meetings on 15 and 16 June.

In fact, Martin Reynolds knows Dang Binh Luan. They met at a World Bank conference the previous year. Two weeks before the meeting, he sent the following e-mail to Dang Binh Luan.

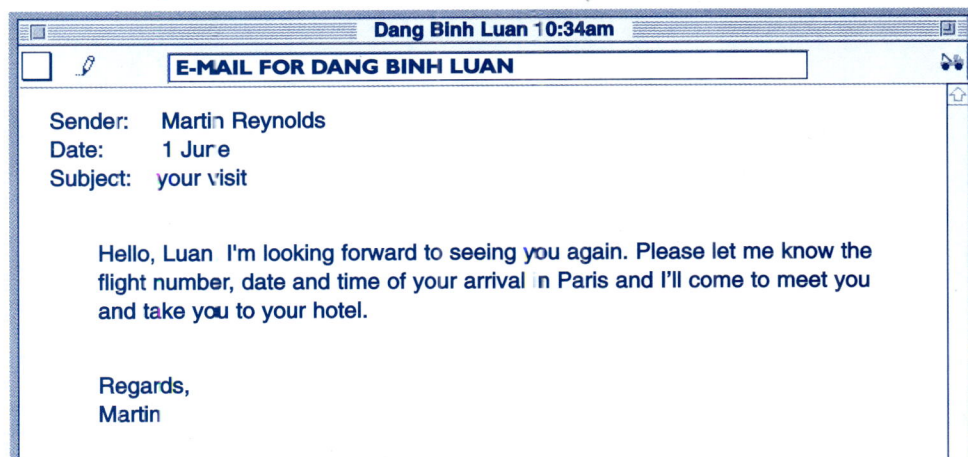

Dang Binh Luan 10:34am

E-MAIL FOR DANG BINH LUAN

Sender: Martin Reynolds
Date: 1 June
Subject: your visit

Hello, Luan I'm looking forward to seeing you again. Please let me know the flight number, date and time of your arrival in Paris and I'll come to meet you and take you to your hotel.

Regards,
Martin

Dang Binh Luan replied by fax. He:
- thanked Martin Reynolds for his offer
- gave his flight details (AF 171 on 14 June; arrival 13.30 at Paris Charles de Gaulle Airport)
- gave his hotel details (Hotel de la Tour, Paris)
- confirmed his appointment at the Asian Investment Bank (15 June at 9.00)

Now write Dang Binh Luan's fax from the notes above. Begin like this:

FAX

FROM: Dang Binh Luan, Ministry of Development, Hanoi, Vietnam
TO: Mr Martin Reynolds, Project Finance Department,
       Asian Investment Bank, Paris
DATE: 2 June
RE: My visit to Paris

Dear Martin

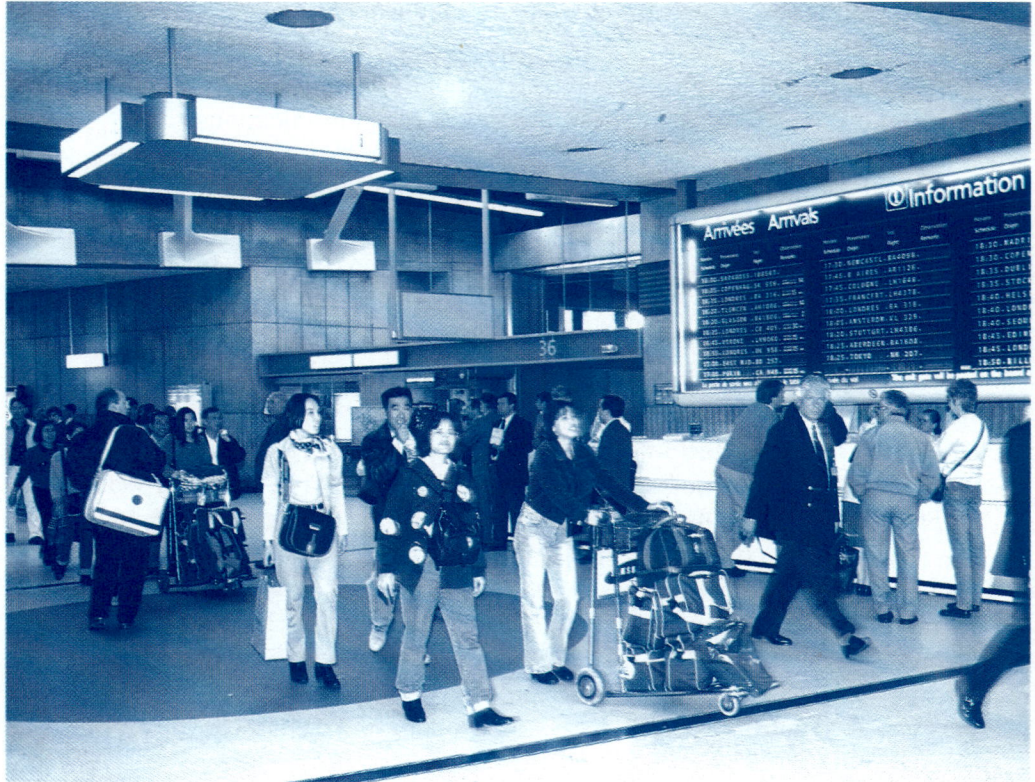

1 🎧 On 14 June, Martin Reynolds was waiting at Paris Charles de Gaulle Airport when he heard a loudspeaker message. Listen to the message, then choose the correct answers.

1 Flight AF 171 will arrive in Paris _____.
   a) early   b) late   c)   on time

2 It will arrive _____.
   a) in the afternoon of 14 June   b) the next day   c) on 16 June

3 Bad weather _____.
   a) stopped the flight in Hanoi   b) delayed the flight
   c) delayed all flights in Europe

2 Flight AF 171 landed at 15.30. The Vietnamese visitors waited for their luggage, then went through customs and passport control and finally met Martin Reynolds in the arrivals lounge.
   Here is part of their conversation. Complete it using the words in the box.

do	how	see	pleased	this

1 Reynolds: Luan! Good to _____ you again.
2 Dang: Hello, Martin. How are you?

3 Reynolds: Fine, thanks. _____ was your flight?

4 Dang: Long and boring, but we're here now. _____ is my colleague, Mr Le Van Nam.

5 Le: How do you _____.

6 Reynolds: _____ to meet you, Mr Le. Right, let's go to my car. It's not far.

3   Martin Reynolds drove his visitors to their hotel, then returned to his office. Listen to the conversation between Dang Binh Luan and the receptionist at the hotel. Then choose the correct answers.

1 Who booked the rooms?
  a) Dang Binh Luan
  b) Martin Reynolds
  c) the Vietnamese embassy in Paris

2 Which type of accommodation was reserved?
  a) two single rooms with bathrooms
  b) a double room with a bathroom
  c) two single rooms with a shower

3 Payment will be made:
  a) immediately
  b) by credit card
  c) by cheque

4 Breakfast is served:
  a) all day
  b) after 7 am in the morning
  c) between 6 and 11 am

5 For dinner:
  a) the restaurant closes at 10 pm
  b) it's not possible to eat in the hotel
  c) the restaurant opens after 10 pm

6 The room numbers are:
  a) 340 and 360
  b) 314 and 360
  c) 314 and 316

4   Now listen again and complete the receptionist's questions.

1 Can _____ _____ _____, sir?

2 May _____ _____ _____ _____, please?

3 And _____ _____ _____ _____ _____ pay, sir?

4 Will _____ ____ _____ breakfast?

5 May _____ _____ _____ _____ luggage?

1 Pair work. Below are the answers to five travel enquiries. Discuss with your partner and write down the corresponding questions. Several questions are possible. The first word is given to help you.

1 Where _____? Departure gate 19, madam.

2 What _____? The check-in time's 15.40.

3 Why _____? Because of bad weather, sir.

4 Can _____? I'm afraid not. It's a no-smoking flight.

5 When _____? The arrival time in London is 18.30.

2 Pair work. Speaker A looks at this page. Speaker B turns to page 76.

Speaker A
Listen to Speaker B and note down the information.

1 Arrival time: _____

2 Flight number: _____

3 Cost of ticket: _____

4 Flight delay: _____

5 Check-in time: _____

Now change roles. Dictate the following sentences to your partner.

1 The flight will take off at 14.30.

2 A return ticket costs 475 euros.

3 The 18.15 flight from Boston is late.

4 The flight number is SW 8174.

5 You must be at the airport by 5.30.

3 Role plays 1 and 2 are both for two students.

Speaker A looks at this page. Speaker B turns to page 77.

SPEAKER A

Role play 1

Le Van Nam wanted to fly back to Vietnam before Dang Binh Luan, who had other appointments in Paris. Neither had reserved his return plane seat.

You are Le Van Nam. You want to leave Paris on 19 June, which is a Friday. Telephone Air France to make your reservation. You want to know:
- the flight number and take-off time
- the duration of the flight
- if there is a film
- the arrival time in Hanoi

Role play 2

Sylvie Lavigne, one of Martin Reynolds's colleagues at the Asian Investment Bank, often travels abroad for meetings.

You are Sylvie Lavigne. You will take part in a meeting at the Scottish Development Bank in Edinburgh on 3 July. You have written the following e-mail to your friend, Jim McBride, who works in Edinburgh. He will telephone you with some information.

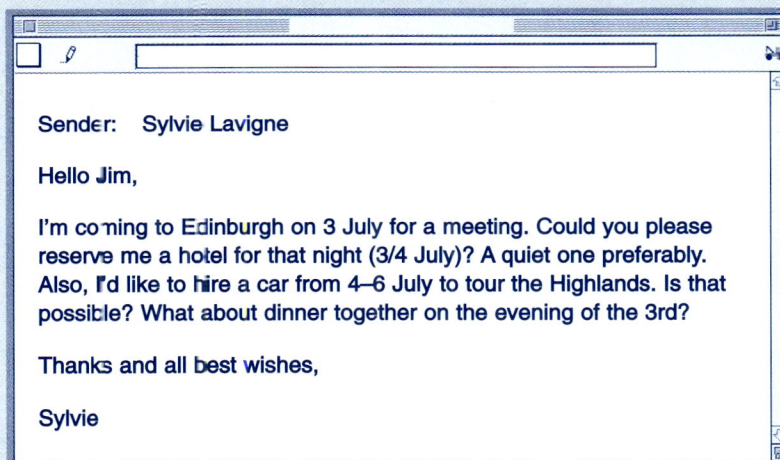

> Sender: Sylvie Lavigne
>
> Hello Jim,
>
> I'm coming to Edinburgh on 3 July for a meeting. Could you please reserve me a hotel for that night (3/4 July)? A quiet one preferably. Also, I'd like to hire a car from 4–6 July to tour the Highlands. Is that possible? What about dinner together on the evening of the 3rd?
>
> Thanks and all best wishes,
>
> Sylvie

4 Work with a partner. You are each going to prepare a short presentation.
Speaker A looks at this page. Speaker B looks at page 77.

SPEAKER A

Presentation

What is important when …?	Useful expressions:
Choosing a hotel	I think that (X) is very important because …
• being close to public transport	
• a good restaurant in the hotel	I don't think (Y) is important because …
• a comfortable room	It's really useful to have …

Exchanging information

making telephone calls

leaving messages

asking about products and services

1 Which of these telephone expressions sounds better – A or B?

1 Introducing yourself	A I am ...	B This is ...
2 Asking for someone	A Could I speak to ...?	B I want to speak to ...
3 Asking someone's name	A Who are you please?	B Can I have your name?
4 Asking for a number	A Can you give me your number?	B Give me your your number.
5 Leaving a message	A Give her a message, will you?	B Can I leave a message?
6 Asking for information	A Could you tell me what the menu is?	B Tell me about the menu.

2 The following words in this unit may be new. Check that you understand them.

FOUND – to start a company (*He founded the company in 1998.*)

TAKE PLACE – to happen (*The meeting will take place in Berlin tomorrow.*)

HOLD – to organise or run (*They held the conference yesterday.*)

SOLVE – to find a solution to something (*She solved the problem of late delivery.*)

ABSTRACT – a written summary of a lecture or article.

A Reading and writing

In this unit (as well as in Units 7 and 11) we will look at the following company:

RESEARCH EXCHANGE

Research Exchange was founded by Julia van Dijk, an English woman who lives in the Netherlands. Research Exchange organises international scientific and medical conferences. These normally take place in Utrecht (Netherlands), where the company is based. Research Exchange has five full-time staff and employs temporary staff during the conferences. The full-time staff are:

- Julia van Dijk, Managing Director
- Ellen Bakker, Organisation Manager
- Jan Muller, Sponsorship Manager
- Jennie Carpenter, Secretary and Accommodation Manager
- Wim Lubbers, Social and Leisure Manager

1 Who does what in Research Exchange? Complete the following sentences with the names of the people responsible.

1 _____ looks after hotel arrangements.

2 _____ is responsible for running Research Exchange.

3 _____ deals with companies who may give money to support conferences.

4 _____ arranges speakers, timetables and so on.

5 _____ manages evening and tourist activities.

2 Read this letter that Julia van Dijk received from Professor Anna Jager, a well-known expert on heart disease.

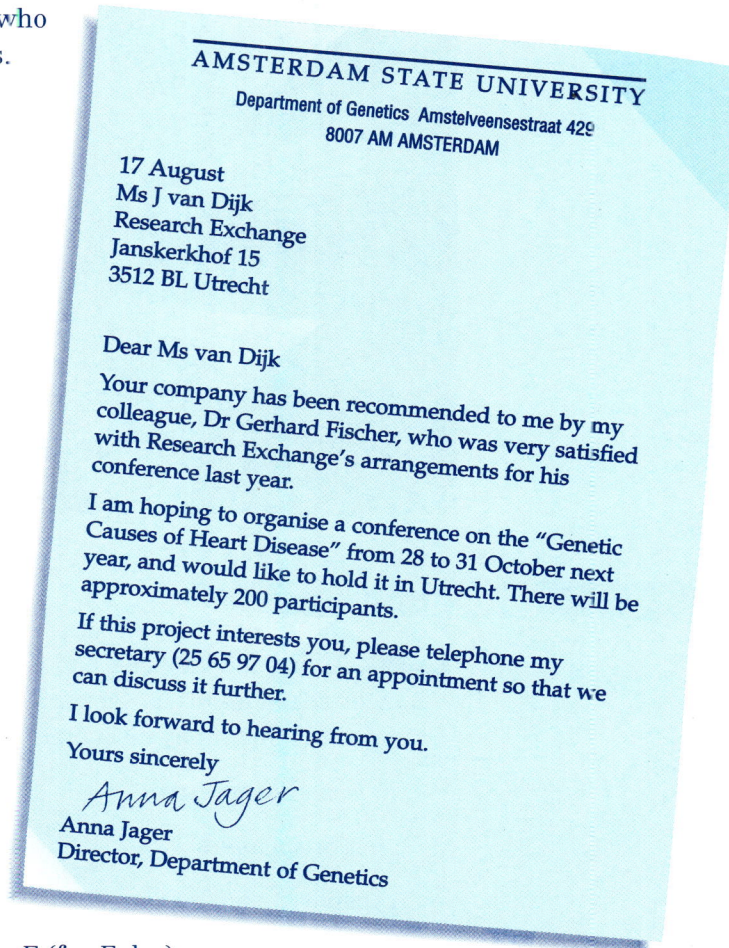

> ### AMSTERDAM STATE UNIVERSITY
> Department of Genetics Amstelveensestraat 429
> 8007 AM AMSTERDAM
>
> 17 August
> Ms J van Dijk
> Research Exchange
> Janskerkhof 15
> 3512 BL Utrecht
>
> Dear Ms van Dijk
>
> Your company has been recommended to me by my colleague, Dr Gerhard Fischer, who was very satisfied with Research Exchange's arrangements for his conference last year.
>
> I am hoping to organise a conference on the "Genetic Causes of Heart Disease" from 28 to 31 October next year, and would like to hold it in Utrecht. There will be approximately 200 participants.
>
> If this project interests you, please telephone my secretary (25 65 97 04) for an appointment so that we can discuss it further.
>
> I look forward to hearing from you.
>
> Yours sincerely
>
> *Anna Jager*
>
> Anna Jager
> Director, Department of Genetics

Now mark these statements T (for True) or F (for False). Correct the sentences you think are false.

1 Gerhard Fischer told Anna Jager about Research Exchange.   T   F
2 Research Exchange has already worked with Anna Jager.   T   F
3 Anna Jager wants Julia van Dijk to come to Amsterdam.   T   F
4 Gerhard Fischer wants to organise a conference next year.   T   F
5 Anna Jager's secretary will contact Julia van Dijk.   T   F

3 Julia van Dijk was interested in Anna Jager's letter and arranged to see her on 4 September. Julia van Dijk began the meeting by explaining the role of Research Exchange and telling Anna Jager what information she needed. Anna Jager took the following notes during the meeting:

> me to provide list of speakers / February at latest
> prepare list of participants / end March
> finalise scientific programme / early April
> visit Conference Centre / JvD to confirm date

The day after their meeting, Anna Jager sent Julia van Dijk an e-mail confirming the points she noted. Use the notes to write her e-mail.

B Listening

1 🎧 After Julia van Dijk had explained the role of Research Exchange, Anna Jager asked about its services. Listen to their conversation and note down the order in which they discussed the different subjects.

the social programme ☐   application forms and accommodation ☐

a list of speakers 1   visa arrangements ☐

transport ☐   sponsorship ☐

a list of participants ☐

2 Listen to the recording again and fill in the missing words.

1 Jager: But now _____ _____ _____ _____ what services Research Exchange offers.

2 van Dijk: Well, basically we _____ _____ _____ everything.

3 van Dijk: _____ _____ _____ I receive a list of the speakers from you, _____ _____ them a letter ...

4 van Dijk: That's it. Research Exchange will _____ _____ their application forms and accommodation.

5 Jager: But who _____ _____ the social programme?

6 van Dijk: We do. _____ you approve the scientific programme, _____ _____ on the social programme together and _____ _____ out a full programme ...

7 van Dijk: Jan Muller is our Sponsorship Manager, so he's _____ _____ that.

8 Jager: Now _____ _____ transport to and from the hotels?

3   Look at the list of tasks below. Listen again and note down if they are the responsibility of:
  • Anna Jager (AJ)   • Research Exchange (RE)   • both sides (both)

provide list of speakers ___AJ___   work on social programme _____

send letter to speakers _____   send out full programme _____

provide list of participants _____   work on sponsorship _____

organise accommodation _____   organise transport _____

approve scientific programme _____

4   🎧 Two weeks after their meeting Anna Jager and Julia van Dijk visited the Utrecht Conference Centre, and Anna Jager decided to hold the conference there.
     The next job was to find hotel accommodation. Julia van Dijk asked Jennie Carpenter to telephone three hotels to enquire about group bookings. These were:
  • the Centraal Hotel in Utrecht
  • the Park Hotel, 15 km from Utrecht
  • the Rembrandt Hotel in Amsterdam, 50 km from Utrecht
     First Jennie Carpenter phoned the Centraal Hotel in Utrecht. Listen to the conversation, then mark the statements T (for True) or F (for False). Correct the sentences you think are false.

1 Jennie Carpenter has spoken to the Centraal Hotel before.   T   F
2 Jennie Carpenter confirms the group booking.   T   F
3 Julia van Dijk will see the hotel manager tomorrow.   T   F
4 Jennie Carpenter will visit the hotel next week.   T   F

5   Choose the correct answers to the following questions.

1 How many rooms will Research Exchange need?
   a) 100 or more   b) fewer than 100   c) approximately 100

2 What date is Julia's appointment with the hotel manager?
   a) Thursday 30th   b) Thursday 13th   c) Tuesday 13th

3 What time is the appointment?
   a) 10.00   b) 09.30   c) 10.30

6   🎧 Next Jennie Carpenter called the Rembrandt Hotel in Amsterdam. Listen to the recording and choose the correct answers.

1 The Rembrandt Hotel: 3 The Rembrandt Hotel:
   a) is only for tourists.   a) is free in October.
   b) does not do conferences.   b) is closed in the winter.
   c) is for tourists in the summer. c) has a conference in October.

2 The Rembrandt Hotel:
   a) has a conference in May.
   b) is full in May.
   c) does not do group bookings.

Finally Research Exchange booked 100 rooms at the Centraal Hotel and 100 rooms at the Park Hotel.

Speaking

1 Pair work. What can you say in the following telephone situations? Practise with a partner.

1 Introducing yourself: *Hello, my name's ...*

2 Asking for someone: _____

3 Asking someone to wait: _____

4 Asking for the caller's name: _____

5 Connecting a caller: _____

6 Asking for repetition: _____

7 Saying someone is not in: _____

8 Leaving a message: _____

2 Pair work. Complete the following telephone conversation with sentences a) to g) below. Then practise the conversation with your partner.

A

Intermed Services. Good morning.

B

Hello. 1 _____

A

I'm afraid she's away this week.
2 _____

B

Yes, please. This is Jim Blakely.
3 _____

A

Certainly. 4 _____

B

B-L-A-K-E-L-Y.

A

Right. 5 _____

B

01237 598461.

A

OK. 6 _____. I'll ask her to call you back next Monday.

B

7 _____.
Bye.

A

Goodbye, Mr Blakely.

a) I've got that.
b) Could you ask her to call me back, please?
c) And your phone number?
d) Fine. Thanks very much.
e) Can I speak to Louise Pagett, please?
f) Can I take a message?
g) Can you spell your name, please?

3   Role plays 1–4 are all for two students.

Early in July, Ellen Bakker was working hard to finalise the conference programme. There were a lot of small problems to be solved, and she had to make and receive a lot of telephone calls.

  Speaker A looks at this page. Speaker B turns to page 78.

Speaker A looks at this page. Speaker B turns to page 78.

SPEAKER A

Role play 1

You are Ellen Bakker.
- Telephone Dr Isabelle Carrier of the Cardiac Research Institute in Paris (France).
- Introduce yourself and explain that you need the title of her presentation.

Role play 2

You are Dr Yukio Matsuhito of the Central Hospital in Kyoto (Japan). Your plane will arrive in Amsterdam late in the evening of 27 October. You are on the programme to give a presentation at 9 o'clock in the morning of 28 October. You want to change the time of your presentation.
- Telephone Ellen Bakker and ask her if this can be done.

Role play 3

You are Ellen Bakker. You want to speak to Dr Li Yang of Number 2 Hospital in Beijing (China). It is urgent.
- Call Dr Li Yang at the hospital.

Useful information:
Your telephone number is 00 31 967 6648.

Role play 4

You are Dr Nelson Nkame, of the University Hospital in Harare (Zimbabwe). You cannot go to the conference yourself, so your place will be taken by a colleague, Dr Margaret Boka.
- Call Ellen Bakker and tell her this.

Meetings and opinions

taking part in meetings

asking for and giving opinions

agreeing and disagreeing

BEFORE YOU START

1 Complete the following sentences using the words in the box.

say	begin	disagree	think	agree	view

1 Opening a meeting   Right, let's _____.

2 Agreeing   I _____ with Tom.

3 Asking for an opinion What do you _____, Charlie?

4 Asking to speak   Can I _____ something here?

5 Giving an opinion   In my _____, ...

6 Disagreeing   I'm sorry, I completely _____.

2 The following words in this unit may be new. Check you understand them.
WEBSITE – a page or pages on the Internet with information or advertising
RECORDING SESSION – making a (musical) recording in a studio
TALENT – an ability to do something (here, musical ability)
TO DOWNLOAD – to transfer data (here, from the Internet onto a computer)

A Reading and writing

In this unit (as well as in Units 8 and 12) we will follow the story of two companies.

magyar ventures Magyar Ventures is a Hungarian software company based in Budapest. It specialises in the development of Internet websites and it also markets and distributes computer equipment. Magyar Ventures often works with foreign companies and has many contacts in Britain, where its technicians have a good reputation.

Macro Music Macro Music is based in central London. It has three main activities – organising concerts, managing music groups and arranging recording sessions. Macro Music employees go to concerts in clubs and bars, where they hope to discover new musical talent. The company operates extensively in France and Germany, but has few activities at present in central Europe.

1 Ilona Tolnai is the Managing Director of Magyar Ventures. She received the lett[er]
page 23 from Macro Music. Read the letter, then mark these statements T (for [True])
or F (for False). Correct the sentences you think are false.

1 Macro Music already sells music through the Internet.	T	F
2 Tom Masters has heard about Magyar Ventures.	T	F
3 He wants to know about the Internet in central Europe.	T	F
4 Tom Masters asks about different sorts of music.	T	F
5 He has already decided to begin the project.	T	F
6 He asks about working with Magyar Ventures.	T	F

4 September

Ms Ilona Tolnai
Magyar Ventures
Roosevelt tér 17
1051 Budapest
Hungary

Macro Music

299 Gerrard Street
LONDON WCI 9XY
tel: 00 44 20 7 358 5823
fax: 00 44 20 7 358 5824
e-mail: macromusic@qnet.co.uk

Dear Ms Tolnai

Our company is well known in the music business in the UK, and we are very interested in the possibilities of the Internet. In fact, one of our projects is the development of websites for the direct sale of music to the general public.

Your company has been recommended to us, and I am writing to find out your views on the following points:

1) In general, what do you think about the future of the Internet for the general public in Hungary and central Europe?
2) In your view, will the downloading of music from the Internet become popular?
3) Which kinds of music will be downloaded (ie popular, classical, jazz, etc)?
4) And finally, if we decide to go ahead with this project, would Magyar Ventures be interested in working with us?

I look forward to receiving your comments in due course.

Yours sincerely

Tom Masters

Tom Masters
Development Manager

2 What did Tom Masters write when he:

1 gave his reason for writing?

_____

2 asked about the future of the Internet?

_____

3 mentioned downloading?

_____

4 asked about kinds of music?

_____

3 Now use the notes on the right to write Ilona Tolnai's reply. Thank Tom Masters for his letter, then give your opinions.

Finish the letter by saying that you would like to meet Tom Masters to discuss possibilities.

– *interesting project / could be profitable in long term*
– *future of Internet: developing quickly*
– *downloading music: already popular / especially with young people*
– *kind of music: 80% popular and jazz / 20% classical*

B Listening

1 🎧 After receiving a reply from Magyar Ventures, Tom Masters decided to meet Ilona Tolnai. They fixed an appointment at the Magyar Ventures office in Budapest.

Listen to part of their conversation and complete the summary using the words in the box.

expensive	drop	interested	at first	classical
short term	secure	popular	yes	optimistic

Ilona Tolnai is very (1) __*optimistic*__ about the Internet possibilities in central Europe, but not in the (2) _____. She thinks that (3) _____ most of the customers will be young people. And although using the Internet is (4) _____ at the moment, she believes that prices will (5) _____ in the near future. Also, she says that the majority of sales will be for (6) _____ music. When Tom Masters suggests special recordings of (7) _____ music on the Internet, she is not sure. They both agree that the website must be simple and (8) _____. When Tom Masters asks if Magyar Ventures is (9) _____ in working with Macro Music, Ilona Tolnai answers (10) _____.

2 Listen to the recording again and fill in the missing words.

1 Tolnai:
   (giving an opinion)
   But I ____think____ it's a long-term investment.

2 Tolnai:
   (agreeing)
   Oh, yes, _____ _____ _____ _____:
   especially in the beginning.

3 Masters:
   (asking for an opinion)
   But _____ _____ be too expensive for them?

4 Tolnai:
   (giving an opinion)
   But _____ _____ prices will fall over the
   next two or three years.

5 Masters:
   (asking for an opinion)
   _____ _____ _____ they would sell on
   the Internet here?

6 Tolnai:
   (giving an opinion)
   _____ _____ _____ it's best to start with
   popular music.

7 Masters:
   (agreeing)
   Hmm ... well, you're _____ _____.

8 Tolnai:
   (giving an opinion)
   Well, _____ _____ _____ it must be as
   simple as possible ...

9 Masters:
   (agreeing)
   Well, that's _____ _____.

10 Tolnai:
   (giving an opinion)
   Yes, Tom. I _____ we can.

3 🎧 Before going to Hungary, Tom Masters had listened to a concert by an
unknown group called The Trainspotters. He had liked their music and asked
them to send a cassette of their songs to Macro Music. After his return from
Budapest, he had a meeting with his boss, Charlie Jennings, as well as Nicci
Garland, the Promotions Manager of Macro Music.
   Listen to their conversation and then mark the statements true or false.
Correct the sentences you think are false.

1 Nicci Garland has listened to The Trainspotters.	T	F
2 She thinks they play well.	T	F
3 Tom Masters agrees with her opinion.	T	F
4 They agree that the singer has some talent.	T	F
5 Charlie Jennings wants to hear them play.	T	F

4 Listen again and fill in the missing words.

1 Nicci Garland did not like The Trainspotters. What did she say about them?

   "_____ _____ _____ _____, Charlie."

2 Tom Masters didn't agree. He said, "They're _____ _____!"

3 Nicci Garland disagreed again. She said, " They've _____ _____

   _____."

4 Tom Masters talked about the singer. He said, "She's got talent, you

   _____ _____ that."

5 Charlie Jennings decided what to do. He said, "Look, _____ _____
   them to come to the studio..."

C Speaking

1 Match the ideas and opinions on the left with the responses on the right.

1 What do you think about the Internet?
2 Do you agree that would be a good market?
3 I think we should start with popular music.
4 She thinks the price is too low.
5 In your view, was that decision correct?

A Yes, I do. Definitely.
B Certainly not.
C Well, she's wrong, in my opinion.
D I think it's going to be very important.
E So do I.

2 Office rents are very high in central London. Charlie Jennings (CJ) and Tom Masters (TM) are discussing how Macro Music can pay less rent. Complete their discussion with sentences a) to h) below.

CJ   TM

1 opens discussion
I think we should move out of London.

2 disagrees and gives reason
_____
_____

3 makes a point
_____
_____

4 makes a point
_____
_____

5 suggests an alternative
_____
_____

6 disagrees
_____
_____

7 makes a suggestion
_____
_____

8 agrees
_____
_____

a) Yes, but office rents are not as expensive outside London.
b) No, Charlie, our offices are already too small.
c) ~~I think we should move out of London.~~
d) Right. Good idea.
e) No, I don't agree. We'd lose contact with our musicians.
f) Why don't we look for smaller offices in London?
g) Let's ask Nicci to look for cheaper offices then.
h) I agree, but the staff want to stay in London.

26

3 Role plays 1 and 2 are both for two students.

After Tom's visit to Budapest there is discussion about which website design company Macro Music should work with.

Speaker A looks at this page. Speaker B turns to page 78.

Role play 1

You are Tom Masters. You are sure that Magyar Ventures is the best company to work with. In your opinion:
- They know the markets in central Europe.
- The technicians of Magyar Ventures have a good reputation.
- Magyar Ventures will be cheaper than British companies.

Discuss your views with Nicci Garland.

Role play 2

You will discuss the possibility of Macro Music organising a "political" rock concert.

You are Nicci Garland. You begin the conversation. You want Macro Music to organise a rock concert against capital punishment. In your opinion:
- It is a good humanitarian cause.
- It would be good for Macro Music's public image
- It would be shown on television internationally.
- Musicians would not ask to be paid.
- Corporate advertising would cover the costs.

4 Work with a partner. You are each going to prepare a short presentation. Speaker A looks at this page. Speaker B looks at page 78.

SPEAKER A

Presentation

What is important when ...?
Attending a business meeting
- being on time
- wearing smart clothes
- good preparation

Useful expressions:
I think that (X) is very important because ...
I don't think (Y) s important because ...
It's really useful to have ...

27

Instructions and warnings

giving instructions

understanding regulations

describing processes

suggesting alternatives

BEFORE YOU START

1 Put the words in these notices and instructions into the correct order.

1 RESPONSIBILITY ACCEPT DO LOSSES NOT WE FOR
2 AFTER PRINTER OFF SWITCH USE
3 HERE CAR YOUR NOT PARK DO
4 TAKE REQUESTED ARE YOU NOT PHOTOGRAPHS TO
5 TEN O'CLOCK PERSONNEL BEFORE MUST ARRIVE
6 CALLS STAFF PERSONAL NOT MUST MAKE
7 ENTRY AUTHORISATION NO WITHOUT

1 *We do not accept responsibility for losses.*

2 _____

3 _____

4 _____

5 _____

6 _____

7 _____

2 The following words in this unit may be new. Check that you understand them.

DELIVERY AND STORAGE AREA – where materials are brought and kept
WAREHOUSE – a building used for keeping goods
ADMINISTRATION BLOCK – general offices
MOULDING – giving shape to something (for example, to hulls and decks)
EXIT – the place where you leave (for example, a building or a highway)
SECURITY – guards who look after people or buildings

A Reading and writing

◀UNIT 1▶ In Unit 1 Manuel Ortega of Polycaracas and Jim Prior of Florida Marine met in Venezuela to talk about possible co-operation. Two months later, Manuel Ortega sent the fax on page 29 to Jim Prior.

1 Read the fax, then mark the following statements true or false. Correct the sentences you think are false.

1 Manuel Ortega plans to go on a business trip. T   F
2 He plans to go to the US in August. T   F
3 He wants to visit the Florida Marine factory. T   F
4 He cannot visit the US in late September. T   F
5 He only wants to see Jim Prior. T   F

FACSIMILE TRANSMISSION

FROM: Manuel Ortega, POLYCARACAS
TO: Mr Jim Prior, Florida Marine
DATE: August 8
RE: Planned visit to Miami

Dear Mr Prior

I was very pleased to see you in Venezuela in June and I hope that your business trip was successful.

I plan to come over to the States next month and would very much like to visit you in Miami. As you can imagine, I am especially interested in your production processes. If Ms Henderson or you are free during the last week of September, would it be possible to arrange an appointment?

Yours sincerely

Manuel Ortega

2 Michelle Henderson faxed a reply to Manuel Ortega. Using the following notes, write her fax.
- thank Manuel Ortega for his fax
- Jim Prior / vacation / September
- you show him / factory
- suggest appointment – September 27 / 9 o'clock
- invite him / lunch / after factory visit
- send him / map with directions / centre of Miami to Florida Marine

3 Look at the map that Michelle Henderson sent. Complete the directions using the verbs in the box.

continue   take
turn   go   take

First (1) _____ Highway 1. Take the first exit after Interstate 195, then (2) _____ right. (3) _____ for two miles along this road until you see a gas station, then

(4) _____ the second turning on the right. (Be careful – the first leads directly to the beach!)

(5) _____ along this road for about a mile and you will see the Florida Marine building on your left.

Notice the words Michelle Henderson used in the instructions (*first, until, then*).

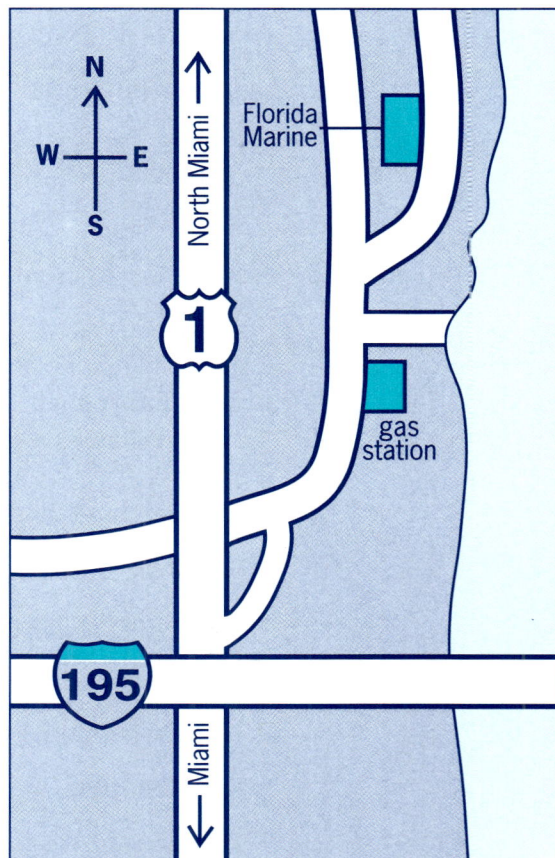

29

1 Manuel Ortega went to visit Michelle Henderson at Florida Marine's headquarters. While they drank coffee in her office, she showed him this map of the factory.

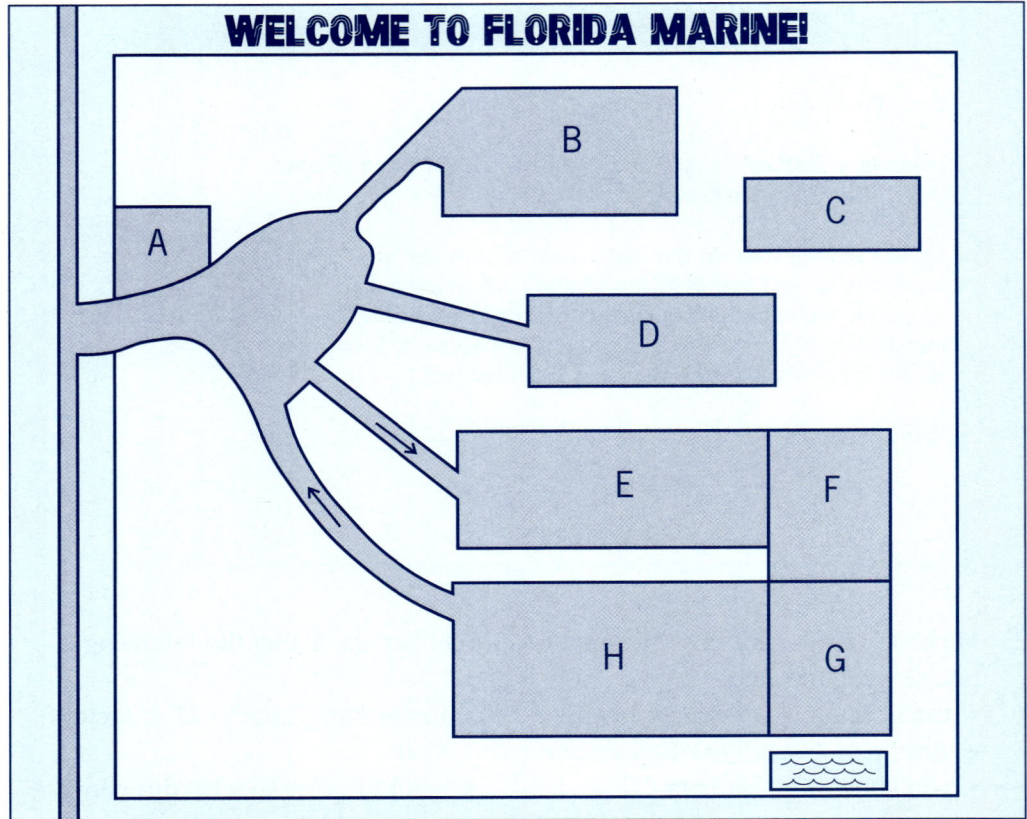

WELCOME TO FLORIDA MARINE!

🎧 Listen to their conversation and write the correct letter (A–H) next to each building or area above. The administration block is letter D on the map.

ADMINISTRATION BLOCK ___D___

SECURITY BUILDING _____

DELIVERY AND STORAGE AREA _____

WAREHOUSE _____

STAFF RESTAURANT _____

MOULDING AREA _____

CAR PARK _____

PAINTING SHOP _____

2 Describe briefly what happens in the following parts of the factory:

1 the delivery area
2 the moulding area
3 the painting shop
4 the warehouse

3 Listen again and fill in the missing words.

1 The first _____ straight to the car park.

2 The factory _____ _____ 24 hours a day.

3 You can see _____ _____ into four sections.

4 That's where the hulls and decks _____ _____.

5 After that they _____ _____, here in the painting shop.

6 The finished boats _____ _____ here, in the warehouse.

4 They left Michelle Henderson's office and began their tour of the factory. After visiting the delivery area they moved on to the moulding area. Florida Marine is very concerned about safety, and there are a lot of warning signs on the walls.

Match each sign with its meaning. (Be careful! One of the meanings has no sign.)

1

A NO RUNNING

2

B SAFETY MASKS MUST BE WORN

C NO BOTTLES OR CUPS ALLOWED

3

D HELMETS MUST BE WORN

4

E NO SMOKING

5

F SAFETY GLOVES MUST BE WORN

5 🎧 In the moulding area, Michelle Henderson talked about the boat-building process. She explained that there are three moulding processes. Listen to the recording and say what parts of the boat they concern.

1 _____.

2 _____.

3 _____.

6 Listen again and complete the following descriptions.

1 First a coat of _____ is put into the mould.
  a) wood   b) fibreglass resin   c) special paint

2 The inside of a boat consists of its _____.
  a) deck   b) cabin walls   c) hull

3 The finished boat is first _____.
  a) put into the warehouse   b) tested on the sea   c) tested in water

1 Look at the notice below, then read the dialogue between a guest and a hotel receptionist.

SORRY. CREDIT CARD MACHINE OUT OF ORDER.

Guest: Can I pay by credit card?
Receptionist: I'm afraid the machine's broken down.
Guest: I see. How can I pay my bill, then?
Receptionist: You can pay in cash or by cheque.

Now complete the following enquiries and requests using the words in the box.

call	what	when	like
where	could		

1 I'd _____ a whisky, please.

2 _____ time does the next bus leave?

3 _____ you send a sandwich to room 43, please?

4 _____ does the bar open?

5 Could you _____ me a taxi, please?

6 _____ exactly is the restaurant?

Notice the following expressions for:

EXPLAINING IMPOSSIBILITIES	MAKING SUGGESTIONS
I'm afraid ...	Why don't you ...
I'm sorry, but ...	You can ...

2 Complete the conversation between a guest and a receptionist with phrases a) to h) below.

1 Guest: Is it _possible to book theatre tickets here_ _____?

2 Receptionist: Certainly. But _____.

3 Guest: But it's _____.

4 Receptionist: I see. I'm _____.

5 Guest: Oh, dear. What _____?

6 Receptionist: Why don't _____?

7 Guest: Do _____?

8 Receptionist: Certainly. I'll _____.

a) afraid we can't help you there
b) get it for you
c) ~~possible to book theatre tickets here~~
d) for tonight
e) we only do advance reservations
f) can I do
g) you call the theatre direct
h) you have the number

3 Role plays 1, 2 and 3 are for two speakers.

Speaker A is a client and Speaker B is a hotel receptionist. A wants something and B must explain why it is not possible and suggest an alternative.

Speaker A looks at this page. Speaker B turns to page 79.

SPEAKER A

Role play 1

It is 5.30 pm on a Wednesday evening. You want a drink.

Role play 2

It is 9.10 am. You want to catch the hotel bus to the town centre. You are in a hurry.

Role play 3

It is 9.30 pm. You are in your hotel room and you are hungry. Telephone reception and ask them to send you a sandwich.

Role play 4 is for two speakers.

Speaker A is an employee of Florida Marine and Speaker B is a visitor to the company.

Speaker A looks at this page. Speaker B turns to page 79.

SPEAKER A

Role play 4

You are an employee of Florida Marine. Using the plan below, describe the layout of Florida Marine's offices to your partner (a visitor) and also tell him/her what is done in each department. You are both standing in the reception area. Start like this:

"Well, as you can see, we're in the reception area, where we receive visitors. The reception desk is over there on the left. To your right, you can see the showroom. That's where the boats are displayed. Now if we walk along the corridor ..."

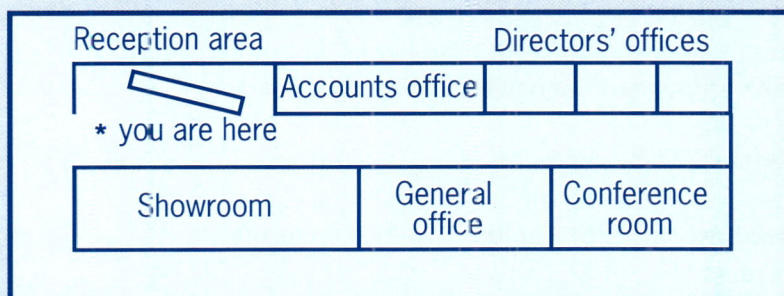

Reception area		Directors' offices			
✳ you are here	Accounts office				
Showroom		General office	Conference room		

Trends and predictions

analysing trends

describing patterns

making predictions

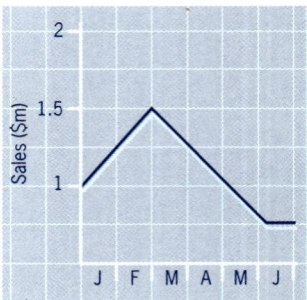

1 The graph on the left shows a company's sales over the last few months. Choose the best words to describe the sales pattern.

1 In January and February sales _____.
a) rose   b) fell   c) levelled out

2 Then they began to _____.
a) go up   b) fall   c) rise

3 In June sales _____.
a) dropped   b) remained level   c) rose

2 The following words may be new. Check that you understand them.
LORRY (AmE TRUCK) – a large commercial vehicle for transporting goods
VAN – a small commercial vehicle
LOAN – money which is lent (usually by banks)
SPONSOR – a person or organisation which gives or lends money
INFLATION – a rise in the cost of living
INVESTMENT – money which is put into projects or companies
RETURN ON INVESTMENT – the profit which investors make

A   Reading and writing

1 Complete the following text, choosing the best word to fill each gap from a), b) or c) below.

INVESTMENT BANKS

Investment banks make loans (1) __to__ organisations or governments

(2) _____ finance particular projects. The loan is repaid with

(3) _____ over a number of years. (4) _____ the sums of

money are sometimes enormous, banks join together to form

(5) _____, and in (6) _____ way they share the (7) _____ in

case anything goes wrong. But the banks do not necessarily (8) _____
the same amounts of money.

1 a) by	b) to	c) at
2 a) to	b) for	c) by
3 a) interest	b) capital	c) profit
4 a) Unless	b) Except	c) As
5 a) unions	b) syndicates	c) companies
6 a) this	b) the	c) those
7 a) profits	b) loans	c) risks
8 a) repay	b) invest	c) give

2 ◀UNIT 2▶ After Dang Binh Luan and Le Van Nam had presented their business plan to the Asian Investment Bank, they returned to Vietnam.

Two weeks later, the Credit Committee of the Asian Investment Bank decided that they could finance part of the project on condition that:
a) a syndicate was formed with the Asian Investment Bank as the sponsoring bank, and
b) a Vietnamese bank was included in the syndicate.

Martin Reynolds wrote a letter to several international investment banks. He gave an outline of the business plan and some background details about the economy of Vietnam. Here is part of his letter.

> Vietnam is economically well-placed in Asia – on the frontier between the mainland and the surrounding south Pacific countries. It has a population of 77 million, which is growing at a rate of 2.26% per year. The capital Hanoi has around 4 million people and Hong Gai (the capital of Quang Ninh province) has over 100,000.
>
> There has been a remarkable rise in foreign investment, from $60 million in 1988 to nearly $2 billion ten years later. With the relaxing of government controls, this trend should continue. The country's industrial growth has risen by an average of around 12% per year since the early 1990s. This is also expected to continue. So we have no doubt that the proposed motorway from Hanoi to Hong Gai will play a major role in developing the economy of Vietnam.
>
> The main financial institutions in Vietnam are

Now complete the following statements.

1 The population of Vietnam _____.
   a) rose by 2.26 million in 1994   b) is increasing   c) is falling

2 Foreign investment in Vietnam has _____.
   a) fallen   b) dropped   c) increased

3 Vietnam's industrial growth _____.
   a) rose by 9% last year   b) went up in the 1990s
   c) went down in the early 1990s

4 The rise in foreign investment _____.
   a) will probably go on   b) will soon stop   c) should slow down

5 The rate of industrial growth _____.
   a) is not expected to change   b) may not continue   c) should slow down

6 Martin Reynolds _____.
   a) doubts the future of a motorway   b) believes in the future of a motorway
   c) does not want to finance a motorway

3 Martin Reynolds received a positive response to his letter from four other investment banks. He was now ready to try to form a syndicate. He asked Sylvie Lavigne to write a short report about the general economic situation of Vietnam. She used the following data for part of her report.

VIETNAM	1992	1995	1999
Inflation (%)	37.5	16.9	7
Exports ($bn)	2.4	5.3	9.8
Lorries (number)	95,123	99,642	104,837

Now write this part of Sylvie Lavigne's report using the data above. Describe the trends in inflation, exports and the number of lorries using the roads.

1 🎧 A few weeks later Sylvie Lavigne flew to Brisbane (Australia) for a meeting with the project finance managers of the Brisbane Investment Bank. Listen to the end of her presentation, then complete the following statements.

1 Sylvie Lavigne _____.
 a) thinks the project will succeed
 b) is not sure about the project
 c) says the project may not be successful

2 To end her presentation she _____.
 a) mentions five major problems
 b) summarises her arguments
 c) says all Asian countries need motorways

2 Listen again and complete the following statements.

1 Since 1994, foreign investment in Vietnam has _____.
 a) fallen   b) remained steady   c) gone up

2 Inflation will probably _____.
 a) rise   b) remain at the same level   c) fall

3 Road transport _____.
 a) is unprofitable   b) will increase   c) will fall

4 Vietnam _____.
 a) suffered from the Asian crisis of 1998
 b) profited from the Asian crisis of 1998
 c) was not affected by the Asian crisis of 1998

5 Sylvie Lavigne says that French banks _____.
 a) have a business advantage in Vietnam
 b) should sponsor cultural links with Vietnam
 c) have little experience of Vietnam

3 Listen to the recording again and fill in Sylvie Lavigne's words.

   1 There has been a _____ _____ of foreign investment.

   2 Inflation is under control and is not _____ to rise.

   3 Road transport _____ _____ increase.

   4 A French-sponsored bank syndicate has _____ _____ _____ of doing business in Vietnam.

4 🎧 After her presentation, Sylvie Lavigne answered several questions. Some were about the growth of lorry, van and bus traffic in Vietnam. Look at the following graph and listen to the recording. Then mark the statements below true or false. Correct the sentences you think are false.

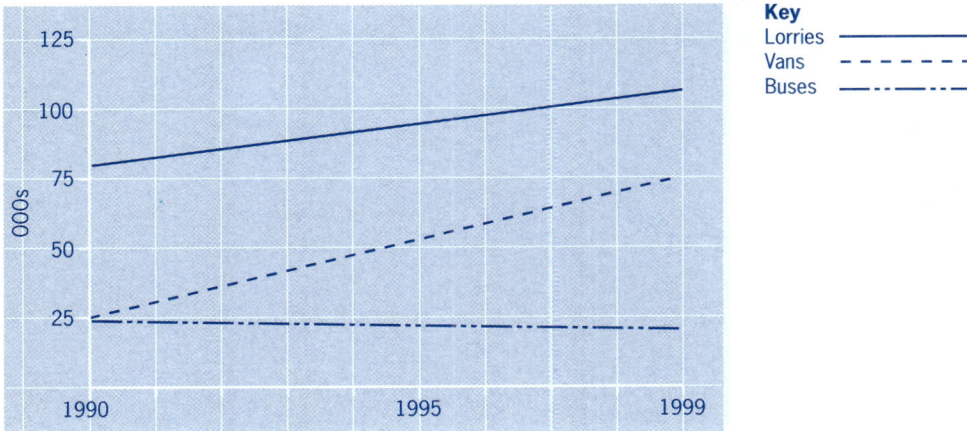

Key
Lorries ——————
Vans – – – – –
Buses —··—··—

(y-axis label: 000s; values 25, 50, 75, 100, 125; x-axis: 1990, 1995, 1999)

   1 Competition from railways has not affected bus traffic.   T   F
   2 Vietnam has 26,000 kilometres of rail track.   T   F
   3 The government modernised its railways in the nineties.   T   F
   4 Van traffic has grown.   T   F
   5 Lorry traffic may go down slightly.   T   F

5 Listen to the recording again and fill in the missing words.

   1 First questioner: I can see that the number of buses _____ _____ during the nineties.

   2 Lavigne: … so the government _____ _____ to use it more in the long term.

   3 Second questioner: The number of vans has _____, hasn't it?

   4 Lavigne: Actually, I'm not sure. But we can be _____ that lorry traffic will _____ _____ over the next few years.

6 Now match the missing words and phrases from Exercise 5 with their equivalents.

   1 went down a little _____

   2 sure _____

   3 increase greatly _____

   4 will possibly want _____

   5 gone up threefold _____

1 Pair work. Speaker A looks at this page. Speaker B turns to page 79.

Speaker A
Look at this graph showing Japanese investment in Vietnam, then describe it to your partner.

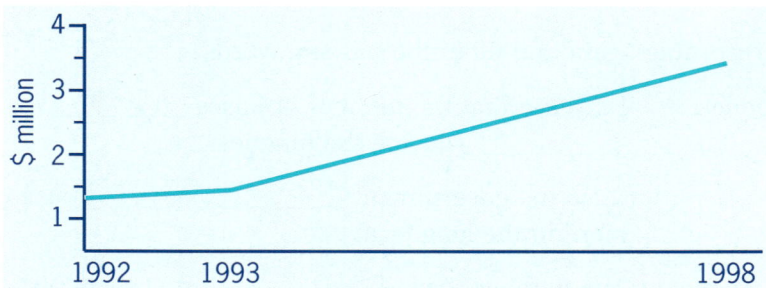

1992	1.34
1993	1.45
1998	3.495

Now listen to your partner. He/she will describe a graph showing Vietnam's industrial growth (in percentage terms) between 1991 and 1998. Fill in the details and then complete the graph.

Year	Figure
_____	_____
_____	_____
_____	_____

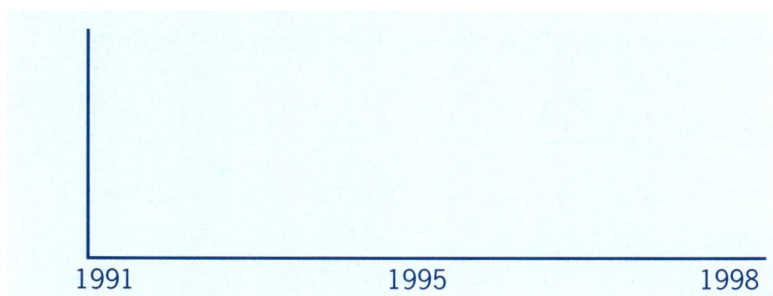

2 Role plays 1 and 2 are for two speakers. They both deal with trends in Japanese society.

Speaker A looks at this page. Speaker B turns to page 80.

Role play 1

You are an expert on Japan. Speaker B will introduce him/herself and then ask you for information about demographic trends in Japan.

- Using the graph on the right and the information below, make a brief presentation to your partner.

Useful information:
Present life expectancy: men – 76.3 years;
women 82.8 years.
At present almost 15% of the population is 65 or over.
Before 2010 one in five Japanese will be a senior citizen.
In 2050 one in three Japanese will be a senior citizen.

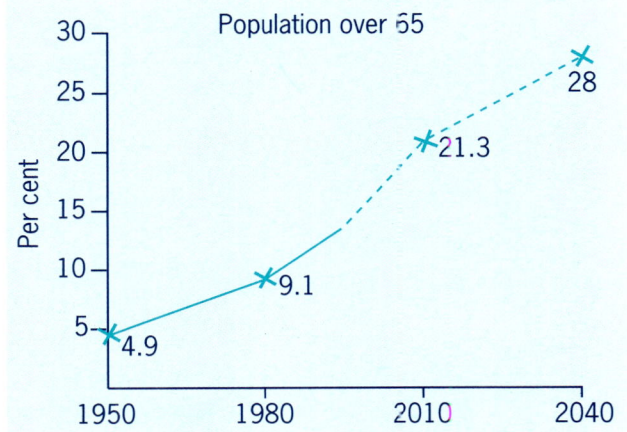

Population over 65

Per cent

30 —
25 —
20 — ✕21.3
15 —
10 — ✕9.1
5 — ✕4.9
✕28

1950   1980   2010   2040

Role play 2

You are an expert on Japan. Speaker B will introduce him/herself and then ask you for information about trends in women's employment.

- Using the graph on the right and the information below, make a brief presentation to your partner.

Useful information:
Women comprise 40% of all employees.
An increasing number of women are well qualified.
About 30% of women do not want to stop working after having children.

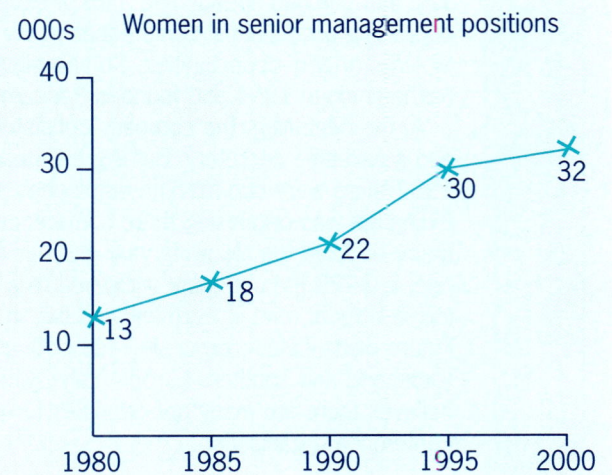

Women in senior management positions

000s

40 —
30 — ✕30   ✕32
20 — ✕22
10 — ✕13   ✕18

1980   1985   1990   1995   2000

Company profiles

describing companies

explaining choices

justifying decisions

A

Volume
20 000

15 000

10 000

5 000

Yr 1   2   3   4   5

B

Volume
20 000

15 000

10 000

5 000

Yr 1   2   3   4   5

BEFORE YOU START

1 Read this description of sales at Alpha Chemicals. Then look at the two graphs on the left. Which one describes Alpha's sales?

> In the first year sales grew rapidly. In the second year they continued to increase, but less quickly. In the third and fourth years sales remained at the same level. In the fifth year they fell and the company was in trouble.

2 The following words in this unit may be new. Check you understand them.
STAND – where companies show their products at conferences
BETA-BLOCKERS – a kind of drug
SUITE – more than one room at a hotel, eg a bedroom, bathroom and
        sitting room
DEPARTMENT STORE – a large shop selling many products
TO ENTERTAIN – to look after visitors and guests
TO RUN – to direct or lead (for example a company, a conference)

A   Reading and writing

Information Pack

Julia van Dijk had already had a lot of experience in organising professional conferences in the UK, and was looking for new opportunities. So she moved to the Netherlands in 1994 and founded Research Exchange.

At the beginning, the company consisted only of Julia and a part-time secretary. But it grew steadily until in 1997 there were two full-time employees and Research Exchange was organising three conferences per year. This figure doubled the following year and has continued to rise. In 1999 the company organised nine conferences (six in Utrecht, one in Germany and two in Belgium). Future plans include expansion into both northern Europe (Denmark) and southern Europe (Italy), where Julia van Dijk believes there are many opportunities for professional conference organisation.

Research E Research Exchange

1 ◀UNIT 3▶ After the conference centre and hotels were arranged, Research Exchange had to organise the details of the conference and look for sponsorship from companies.

Jan Muller, the Sponsorship Manager of Research Exchange, wrote to several large drug companies to inform them about the conference. He sent an information pack with his letter. Here is the first page, which introduces Research Exchange.

Mark these statements true or false. Correct the sentences you think are false.

1 Julia van Dijk ran conferences in the UK.		T	F
2 At the start, Julia van Dijk worked alone.		T	F
3 Julia van Dijk's staff worked full time in 1997.		T	F
4 In 1998 Research Exchange organised six conferences.		T	F
5 In 1999 Research Exchange ran six conferences outside the Netherlands.		T	F
6 Research Exchange may expand into Denmark or Italy.		T	F

2 Complete the following sentences using the correct form of the verbs in the box.

| run | perform | consist of | expand | found |

1 Research Exchange _____ very well in 1999.

2 He _____ the department efficiently.

3 The company was _____ in 1994.

4 At present Research Exchange _____ five full-time staff.

5 She hopes to _____ into Denmark.

3 You are Ingrid Bendt, the Public Relations Manager of the large drug company Pharmasynthesis in Berne (Switzerland). Your company has decided to take part in the conference, and you have been asked to look after the details. First look at your company's requirements, then fill in the form from Research Exchange below.

PHARMASYNTHESIS REQUIRES:
- **stand**
- **meeting room for commercial presentation**
(preferably on 29/10 am or 30/10 pm)
- **presentation:**
title *"Beyond beta-blockers"*
video cassette player required
- **hotel accommodation:**
preferably in centre of town; for three people
number of rooms: 2 singles, 1 suite
participants' names: Professor Johannes Klein (suite)
Dr Marie-Laure Foucault
Ms Ingrid Bendt

COMPANY PRESENTATIONS AND ACCOMMODATION

CONFERENCE: "Genetic Causes of Heart Disease"

Please complete this form and return it to Ellen Bakker at Research Exchange (Fax: 00 31 20 849301)

CONFERENCE REQUIREMENTS

1 If you require a stand, please tick here: ☐

2 If you wish to give a commercial presentation, please complete the following:

The title: _____

Preferred times (circle, giving two preferences)

29/10 morning   30/10 morning   31/10 morning

29/10 afternoon   30/10 afternoon

Meeting rooms are equipped with microphones and overhead projectors. If you need any other equipment, please specify below:

_____

ACCOMMODATION REQUIREMENTS

3 Please note below the full names and titles of all participants:

Surname	First name	Title
_____	_____	_____
_____	_____	_____
_____	_____	_____

4 Please underline the name of the hotel required:
the Centraal Hotel   the Park Hotel
Number/type of accommodation required:
single room(s) __ double room(s) __ suite(s) __

Research Exchange

1 🎧 Ellen Bakker received the application form from Pharmasynthesis in May. She gave a copy to Jennie Carpenter for the hotel accommodation requirements.

The Centraal Hotel, in the centre of Utrecht, was more popular than the Park Hotel, which was 15 km away. Jennie Carpenter telephoned Ingrid Bendt to discuss two problems. Listen to part of their conversation, then complete the following statements.

1 The first problem is about _____.
   a) rooms at the hotel
   b) the application form
   c) other participants

2 Jennie Carpenter suggests _____.
   a) they travel by bus
   b) another hotel
   c) they stay in the centre of town

3 The second problem is about _____.
   a) Professor Klein's visitors
   b) the Excelsior Hotel
   c) Professor Klein's accommodation

4 Professor Klein wants to stay in the centre of town because _____
   a) he likes parties
   b) he has to meet other participants socially
   c) he doesn't like single rooms

5 The Excelsior Hotel _____.
   a) has no single rooms
   b) has no suites
   c) costs a lot of money

2 Now answer the following questions.

1 What is the cause of the first problem?
2 What does Jennie Carpenter say about the Park Hotel?
3 What is the second problem?
4 Why is the second problem important?
5 How does Ingrid Bendt summarise the choice? Fill in the missing words:
   "So it's _____ a single room at the Park _____ a suite at the Excelsior?"
6 What does Ingrid Bendt ask Jennie Carpenter to do?

3 Ellen Bakker also had problems with the application form from Pharmasynthesis. First read the e-mail she sent to Ingrid Bendt:

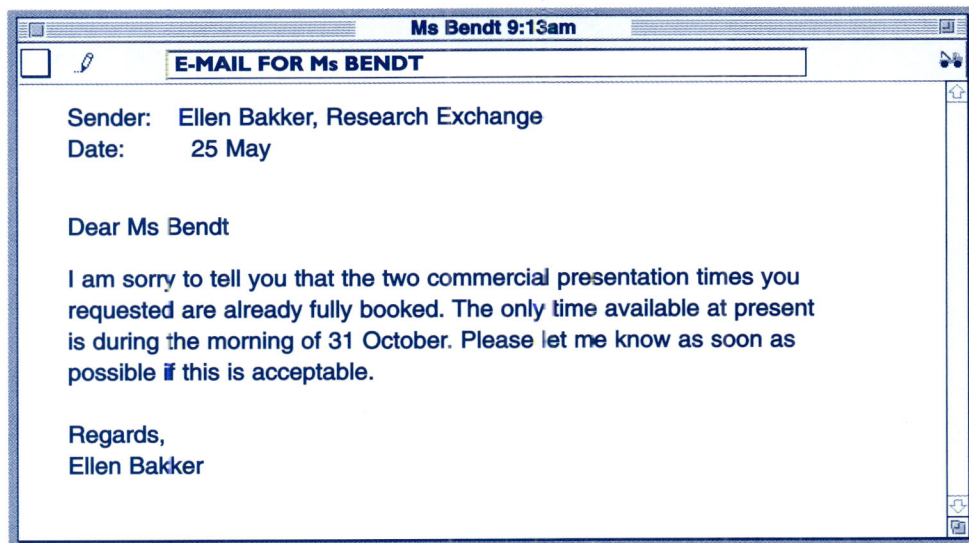

Ms Bendt 9:13am

E-MAIL FOR Ms BENDT

Sender: Ellen Bakker, Research Exchange
Date: 25 May

Dear Ms Bendt

I am sorry to tell you that the two commercial presentation times you requested are already fully booked. The only time available at present is during the morning of 31 October. Please let me know as soon as possible if this is acceptable.

Regards,
Ellen Bakker

When she received this e-mail, Ingrid Bendt telephoned Ellen Bakker. Listen to their conversation and answer the questions.

1 Why doesn't Ingrid Bendt want 31 October?
2 How does Ellen Bakker explain her decision?
3 What does Ellen Bakker suggest?

4 Listen again and fill in the expressions that Ellen Bakker used during the conversation.

1 (Clarifying a situation) I'm afraid so. _____ _____, all the other presentation times are already reserved ...

2 (Explaining a problem) I know, Ms Bendt. _____ _____

   _____ _____, we've only just received your application form.

3 (Justifying a decision) Other companies sent their forms in two or three months ago, _____ _____ they had priority.

4 (Suggesting a solution) _____, I'll reserve you a place for 31 October, but _____ _____ a cancellation for the other days, _____ contact you immediately.

5 (Agreeing) _____. I'll send it today.

5 Now write the e-mail that Ellen Bakker sent to Ingrid Bendt.

Speaking

1 Circle the "odd one out" below.

1 found (relocate) start

2 take over   buy   employ

3 move   sell   relocate

4 buy   export   sell abroad

5 start   run   manage

6 change job   stop working   retire

7 cut   reduce   raise

8 stay   leave   remain

2 Look at the following notes about the development of a British company called Norton Medicines. Match the notes (1–8) with the full sentences (a–h) below.

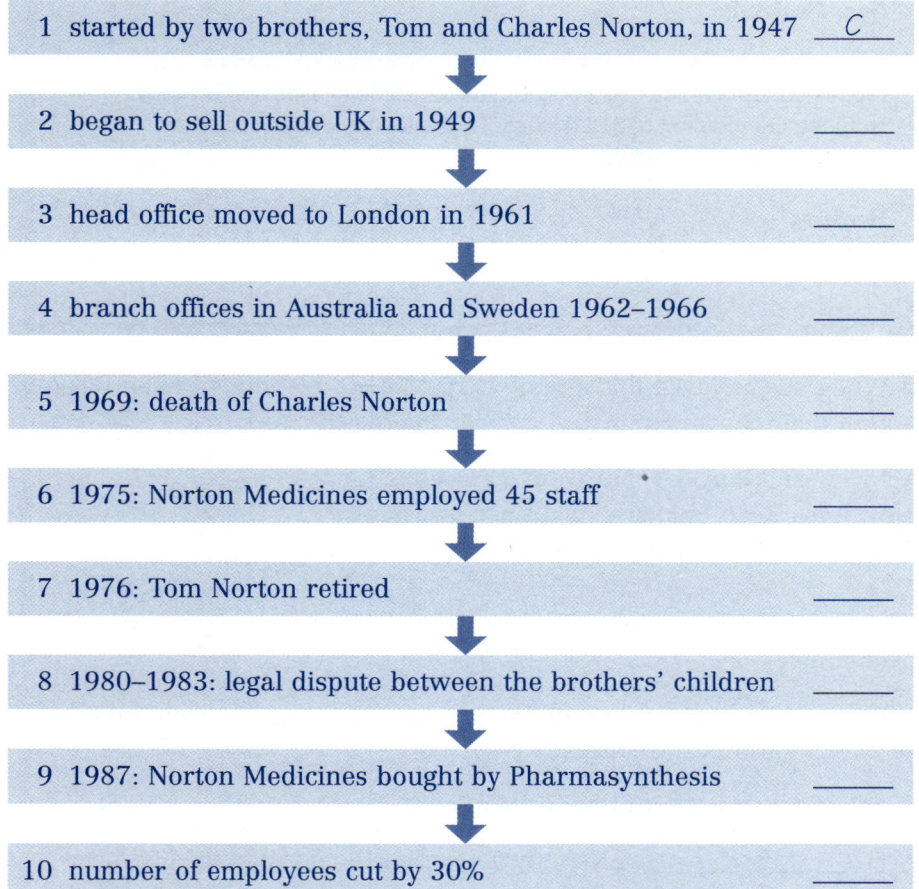

1 started by two brothers, Tom and Charles Norton, in 1947 ___C___

2 began to sell outside UK in 1949 _____

3 head office moved to London in 1961 _____

4 branch offices in Australia and Sweden 1962–1966 _____

5 1969: death of Charles Norton _____

6 1975: Norton Medicines employed 45 staff _____

7 1976: Tom Norton retired _____

8 1980–1983: legal dispute between the brothers' children _____

9 1987: Norton Medicines bought by Pharmasynthesis _____

10 number of employees cut by 30% _____

a) Soon after, offices were opened abroad.
b) Then one of the brothers died.
c) The company was founded by two brothers.
d) The company was taken over in the late 1980s.
e) After the takeover only 28 of the original staff remained.
f) Two years later, Norton Medicines started to export.
g) In the early 1980s there were legal problems.
h) In the mid 1970s Norton Medicines had nearly 50 employees.
i) The company moved at the beginning of the 1960s.
j) The other brother ran the company alone for seven years.

3 Role play 1 is for two speakers.

Karnak Stores is a Swedish group of department stores. It wants to open a new store in Bratislava (Slovak Republic).

Speaker A looks at this page. Speaker B turns to page 81.

Speaker A looks at this page. Speaker B turns to page 81.

SPEAKER A

Role play 1

You are the Investment Manager of Karnak Stores. You have come to Bratislava to present your company to some government officials.
• Prepare your presentation, then make it. Be ready to answer any questions.

Notes:
Karnak Stores founded / Stockholm / 1952
1959: 50 employees
second store opened / Oslo (Norway) / 1962
1963–1980: expansion / western Europe
1997: store opened / Warsaw (Poland)
now: 15 stores / Europe / total 2,600 employees

You can offer:
– about 60 jobs (mainly sales assistants)
– good salaries and working conditions
– opportunities for Slovak suppliers

Useful information:
The company language is English.
Training will be given to managers.
You want to open in the centre of town.
You want to open in two years' time.

Role play 2 is for two speakers.

Zahn Technik is a German company that makes dental equipment. It wants to sponsor a one-day conference at the Utrecht Conference Centre. The executives of Zahn Technik have asked the Director of the Utrecht Conference Centre (UCC) to make a short presentation.

Speaker A looks at this page. Speaker B turns to page 81.

SPEAKER A

Role play 2

You are the Director of the Utrecht Conference Centre. You will present your organisation and explain what you can offer.

Notes:
UCC founded / 1989
early 1990s: average 10 conferences per year
biggest conference: 280 participants / last year
now: average 20 conferences per year

You can offer:
– meeting rooms (large and small)
– audio-visual equipment
– excellent food and facilities

Useful information:
International phones, fax, e-mail and Internet are available.
Meeting rooms are 35 and 75 square metres.
There is no sleeping accommodation.

UNIT 8

Suggestions and reasons

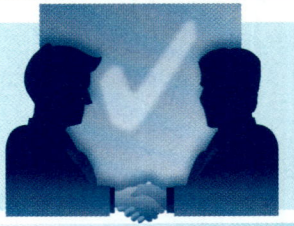

making suggestions

suggesting alternatives

justifying decisions

giving reasons

1 Make suggestions using the correct form of the verbs in the box.

> not/record   ask   advertise   not/begin   open

1 We really should _____ an office in Bucharest.

2 Why _____ we _____ advertising in July?

3 Why _____ we _____ a classical concert?

4 We could _____ on the radio.

5 Let's _____ Macro Music for finance.

2 The following words in this unit may be new. Check that you understand them.
PERFORMANCE – playing to an audience
TV AND RADIO SPOTS – short appearances on TV and radio
COPYRIGHT – legal rights to an original work, eg a book or piece of music

A Reading and writing

1 ◄ **UNIT 4** ▶ In the weeks that followed Tom Masters's visit to Budapest, he finalised an agreement with Magyar Ventures and signed a recording contract with The Trainspotters. He was also planning a third project. Read the letter on page 47 which he wrote to Gustav Richter, the manager of the Wienbad Youth Orchestra in Austria. Then complete the statements below.

1 Internet sales of music _____.
   a) will probably rise
   b) already represent 30% of music sales
   c) are made by experts

2 The Wienbad Youth Orchestra is _____.
   a) very profitable
   b) getting larger
   c) becoming more popular

3 Tom Masters wants the Wienbad Youth Orchestra to _____.
   a) perform in public
   b) make a CD
   c) record for the Internet

4 He suggests recording _____.
   a) songs from different countries
   b) ten Austrian songs
   c) a complete opera

29 October

Mr G. Richter
Wienbad Youth Orchestra
Am Hofgarten 65
1626 Vienna
Austria

Macro Music

299 Gerrard Street
LONDON WC1 9XY
tel: 00 44 20 7 358 5823
fax: 00 44 20 7 358 5824
e-mail: macromusic@qnet.co.uk

Dear Mr Richter

As you probably know, experts think that in the next ten years about 30% of music sales will be made over the Internet. At Macro Music we are very interested in these developments.

It is our policy to promote new musical talent of all types. The popularity of the Wienbad Youth Orchestra is growing, and we believe that collaboration between yourselves and Macro Music could be very profitable for both of us.

What we suggest is a copyrighted performance that can be sold directly over the Internet. Obviously the choice of music will have to be discussed, but in our opinion it should be popular and easy to recognise. For example, we could sell a very attractive collection of about ten songs from European countries, performed by well-known singers from each country. Alternatively we could record parts of operas or Viennese waltzes.

We know that many orchestras are facing financial difficulties at present, but we believe that by co-operation with companies like Macro Music, these difficulties can be solved.

I hope these ideas will be of interest, and I look forward to hearing from you.

Yours sincerely

Tom Masters

Tom Masters
Development Manager

2 In the third paragraph of his letter, Tom Masters made three suggestions. Read the paragraph again and note below the language he used.

1 _____

2 _____

3 _____

3 After receiving the letter from Macro Music, Gustav Richter had a meeting with the conductor and some of the musicians of the Wienbad Youth Orchestra. Here are the notes he took during the meeting:

From these notes, write the reply that Gustav Richter sent to Tom Masters.

AGREE: copyrighted performance/ Internet
SUGGEST: CD sales as well
DISAGREE: songs and waltzes
REASON: not original
SUGGEST: performance of film music
ALTERNATIVE: selections from Duke Ellington
REASON: more interesting/young people

Listening

1 🎧 Three weeks later, Macro Music decided to negotiate a contract with The Trainspotters.

Listen to the conversation between Rico (the lead guitarist of The Trainspotters), Nicci Garland and Tom Masters.

Which of the following subjects do they discuss, and in what order?

transport
meals   1 _____
accommodation   2 _____
money
number of concerts   3 _____
security

2 Match the following words with their meanings.

1 clause	A	a legal agreement
2 specify	B	part of a contract
3 contract	C	to make a condition in a contract

3 Listen again. Complete each statement. Then note down the results of the negotiation.

1 Clause 4 specifies _____.
  a) ten concerts a month
  b) concerts for three weeks
  c) concerts at weekends

2 They agree on _____.

SUGGESTIONS AND REASONS **8**

3 Clause 5 specifies _____.
   a) single rooms in cheap hotels
   b) double rooms in good hotels
   c) double rooms in cheap hotels

4 They agree on _____.

5 Clause 6 specifies _____.
   a) £240 per week per musician
   b) £60 per week per musician
   c) a fixed amount for each concert

6 The pay is _____ per musician per _____.

4 Now listen again and fill in the missing words.

1 Garland: Well, how many _____ _____ _____, Rico?

2 Rico: _____ _____ eight a month?

3 Garland: _____ _____, Rico, Macro Music isn't a rich company.

4 Garland: _____ it's _____ double rooms in good hotels _____ single rooms in cheap hotels.

5 Masters: Clause 6. _____ _____ a fixed amount per concert.

6 Garland: _____ _____, you're not the Rolling Stones.

5 🎧 A few days before the beginning of The Trainspotters' UK tour Nicci Garland received a telephone call from Frankie Black, a journalist from Music World.
   Listen to their conversation and mark the statements true or false.

1 Nicci Garland knows Frankie Black.	T	F
2 Frankie Black wants to interview only Alex.	T	F
3 At the moment The Trainspotters are on holiday.	T	F
4 Frankie Black wants to sell CDs.	T	F
5 Frankie Black offers free publicity to Nicci Garland.	T	F
6 Nicci Garland agrees to an interview on Monday.	T	F

6 Listen again and note the different suggestions and the reasons that are given.

1 Garland: It's difficult at the moment *because* _____

   _____

2 Black: All groups need publicity, *that's how* _____

   _____

3 Black: Look, *supposing* _____

   _____

4 Black: *That way* you get _____

5 Garland: Yes, OK then. *What about* _____?

6 Black: *You see*, I usually _____

7 Black: *Couldn't we make it* _____?

1 Correct the following sentences.

1 I suggest to start with the American market.
2 In order sell CDs we must advertise.
3 We could to ask for Gustav Richter's opinion.
4 It's impossible to open an office there because high rents.
5 Why don't we to organise a concert in Prague?

2 Giving reasons and justifying. Complete the sentences using words or phrases from the box.

because	in order to	that way	so	because of

1 We need television __in order to__ advertise our products.

2 Our website must be clear _____ that users will understand it.

3 We must also sell CDs _____ some customers don't have computers.

4 Let's advertise on radio. _____ we'll increase sales.

5 We must have a secure system _____ computer fraud.

3 Role play 1 is for two speakers.

It is December. Gustav Richter has come to London to discuss collaboration on an Internet recording with Tom Masters. They have decided to record film music, but no other details have been agreed.

Before doing the first role play, reread Section A of this unit to review the situation between Macro Music and the Wienbad Youth Orchestra.

Speaker A looks at this page. Speaker B turns to page 81.

SPEAKER A

Role play 1

You are Tom Masters. You begin the meeting. Note down what you agree.
You want:
- to record American film music (more popular)
- the recordings to be next May/June, possibly July
- the advertising budget to be shared 50/50 (Macro Music cannot pay it all)
- sponsorship from Austrian and UK banks and insurance companies (good for their public image)

After the role play, write a letter from Tom Masters to Gustav Richter confirming the terms of your agreement.

Role play 2 is for two speakers.

Over the last few months, Macro Music has invested a lot of money in its project with Magyar Ventures, and now it is facing financial difficulties. Charlie Jennings has arranged a meeting with Tom Masters to decide how Macro Music's costs can be cut.

Speaker A looks at this page. Speaker B turns to page 81.

SPEAKER A

Role play 2

You are Charlie Jennings.
- Tell Tom Masters that total costs must be cut by 20%.
- Agree with him how this could be done.
  Here is a breakdown of current costs, which add up to £450,000 a year.

Staff costs (salaries)	% of total costs
Directors (3)	25%
Administrative staff (4)	15%
Drivers (2)	10%
Publicist (1)	5%
Trainee (1)	2%

Other costs	
Studios	10%
Advertising	20%
Travel & accommodation	10%
General	3%

Terms of sale and delivery

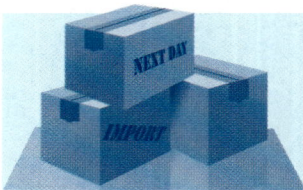

negotiating terms of sale

agreeing delivery dates

making decisions

BEFORE YOU START

1 Match the following questions with their answers.

1 What discounts can you offer?	A Most of our materials come from Brazilian companies.
2 How long is your delivery time?	
3 Who are your major suppliers?	B Yes, if you can guarantee quality.
4 Do you agree to a three-year contract?	C That depends on how much you buy.
5 Can you guarantee regular orders?	D Ten days at the most.
	E We'd prefer an annual one.

2 The following words in this unit may be new. Check that you understand them.

DRUM – a metal container, similar to a barrel

DISCOUNT – a reduction in the price of a product

CANOE – a boat for one or two persons

SUPPLIER – a person or company who provides other companies with materials or services

A Reading and writing

1 ◄UNIT 5► Complete the following text using the words in the box.

> contract   staff   supplier   manager
> year   hired   equipment   factory

After his first visit to Venezuela in June, Jim Prior decided that Florida Marine would move into Venezuela in the spring of the following (1) _____. First he rented a small (2) _____ near Caracas, then he (3) _____ Francisco Cordoves, a Venezuelan, to be the factory (4) _____. Francisco Cordoves was given the job of buying (5) _____ for the factory and finding qualified (6) _____.

In October Jim Prior returned to Caracas with his Finance Manager, Jack Ramsey. They had an appointment to meet Manuel Ortega, Managing Director of Polycaracas, as a possible (7) _____ of fibreglass resins. But before signing a (8) _____, they had to discuss terms of sale, delivery dates and, of course, prices.

2   Mark these statements true or false. Correct the sentences you think are false.

1 By October, Florida Marine's factory was already working.   T   F
2 The factory is in Caracas.   T   F
3 Florida Marine's manager in Venezuela is not American.   T   F
4 Jim Prior hired Florida Marine's staff in Venezuela.   T   F
5 Jim Prior returned to Venezuela in the autumn.   T   F
6 Jim Prior has already signed a contract with Polycaracas.   T   F

3   Look at this price list and fill in the missing information from the sentences below.

PRICE LIST – FIBREGLASS RESINS   POLYCARACAS
(prices in US dollars)

Type of resin	100 kg drum	250 kg drum	Type of boat
VENELITE		410	
PRIMAGLASS	190		12-metre boats
VENEMIX		520	

1 A small drum of Venelite costs 170 dollars.
2 A large drum of Primaglass costs 270 dollars more than a small one.
3 One hundred kilos of Venemix is 50 dollars more expensive than a small drum of Venelite.
4 The cheapest resin is used for small boats and canoes.
5 Motor boats are made with a resin that costs 220 dollars per 100 kg drum.

4   A few days before his flight, Jim Prior made notes of several questions he wanted to ask about prices, terms of sale and delivery. Here are his notes.

what discount / Venelite?
use / Primaglass / canoes?
payment 90 days after delivery?
possible / reduction / Venemix?
guarantee minimum delivery time?
contract: 1 year?

Using these notes, he then sent an e-mail to Francisco Cordoves asking for comments. Complete the e-mail he sent.

Francisco Cordoves 17:07pm

E-MAIL FOR FRANCISCO CORDOVES

To: Francisco Cordoves /francisc@flomarine.com/
Sender: Jim Prior /jimp@flomarine.com/
Date: 10/13

Hi, Francisco

Here are some things I want to ask Mr Ortega at the meeting. Have I forgotten anything?
Let me have your comments, please.

Listening

1 🎧 On the evening before the meeting in Caracas, Jim Prior, Jack Ramsey and Francisco Cordoves had dinner in a restaurant.

First look at the words and phrases in the box. Then listen to the recording and tick [✓] the words you hear.

Venemix	☐	motor boats	☐
wine	☐	discounts	☐
supplier	☐	quality	☐
Chile	☐	tomorrow	☐
steak	☐		

2 What did they say? What did ...

1 Jack Ramsey say about Chilean wine?

_____

2 Francisco Cordoves say about the wine?

_____

3 Jack Ramsey say about quality?

_____

4 Francisco Cordoves say about Polycaracas?

_____

5 Jim Prior say about quality?

_____

3 Listen again and fill in the missing words.

1 Prior: Well, Francisco, you know we're _____ _____ _____ the Primaglass resin.

2 Prior: Not in the _____ _____. We'll only build 12-metre boats to begin with.

3 Ramsey: The _____ _____ for the _____ quality. That's what we always want.

4 Cordoves: Well, Polycaracas isn't necessarily the _____ supplier, but they're _____.

5 Ramsey: Hmm. What do you think about _____ _____, Francisco?

4 🎧 The next day they arrived at Polycaracas. Jim Prior introduced his colleagues to Manuel Ortega, then the meeting began.

Listen to the first part of the conversation and choose the correct phrase.

1 Ortega: *(opening the meeting)*
Right, gentlemen. _____.
a) Shall we start?   b) Let's start.

2 Prior: *(explaining)*
               And today _____ to work out details.
               a) we're here to try   b) we've got to try

3 Ortega: *(asking for information)*
               OK, but first _____ when you plan to open ...
               a) I want to know   b) I'd like to know

4 Prior: *(replying)*
               Right. Jack, can you _____ that?
               a) tell Mr Ortega about   b) fill Mr Ortega in on

5 Ramsey: *(explaining)*
               Sure. Well, _____ production in about six months.
               a) we hope to start   b) we plan to begin

5 🎧 Listen to the second part of the conversation and complete the statements.

1 At first Manuel Ortega believes that Florida Marine will buy

   _____.
   a) Primaglass for a month
   b) the same amount of Primaglass every month
   c) different quantities of Primaglass every year

2 Jim Prior wants to buy _____.
   a) 1,000 kg a month
   b) 2,000 kg a month for three months
   c) 6,000 kg a year

3 Polycaracas can deliver the resin _____.
   a) in three days if it's in stock
   b) only in fixed quantities
   c) immediately after the order

4 Jim Prior _____.
   a) agrees to a monthly fixed order
   b) wants a guarantee about stock
   c) makes no decision about quantities

6 Complete this summary of the conversation using the words in the box.

stock   fixed   rise   guarantee   days   orders   first

Florida Marine wants to buy the Primaglass resin, but not in

(1) _____ quantities. The amount will (2) _____ to 5,000

or 6,000 kg per month by the end of the (3) _____ year. Delivery time

is three (4) _____ on condition that Primaglass is in

(5) _____. Manuel Ortega promises that if Florida Marine

(6) _____ a fixed quantity per month, he will (7) _____ a

three-day delivery time.

Unfortunately, they did not have time to reach an agreement about prices and discounts, so Jim Prior promised to telephone Manuel Ortega the next day to discuss them.

1 Complete the following sentences using a preposition from the box.

in	by	on	to	of

1 We offer a discount _____ 7%.

2 We will deliver _____ two weeks.

3 You will have the goods _____ Thursday at the latest.

4 Can you deliver the resins directly _____ our factory?

5 OK, we'll meet _____ Wednesday to discuss prices.

2 Match the following offers with the correct responses.

1 We can offer a 3% discount.	A Well, 1,000 kg a month, for example.
2 Delivery time is ten days.	B Yes, if the resin's in stock.
3 Our price is $250 a drum.	C Mostly Brazilian companies.
4 What's a fixed quantity?	D I'd prefer a yearly one.
5 Is delivery fast?	E It's very expensive.
6 I suggest a two-year contract.	F Once a month usually.
7 How often do you deliver?	G I'd prefer 5%.
8 Who are your suppliers?	H That's a long time.

3 Role play 1 is for two speakers.

Jim Prior and Manuel Ortega are discussing prices and discounts over the phone.

Speaker A looks at this page. Speaker B turns to page 82.

SPEAKER A

Role play 1

You are Jim Prior. Florida Marine will order 3,000 kg of Primaglass per month for a year at a base price of $190 per 100 kg.
- Telephone Manuel Ortega with your offer. You want the following conditions:
  – discount: 6.5%
  – if you order more than 3,000 kg a month, extra discount of 3%
  – delivery in three days
- Note down what you agree.

Now write a fax from Jim Prior to Manuel Ortega, confirming what you have agreed.

Role play 2 is for two speakers.

It is now six months later. Boat sales have been very good recently and Florida Marine (Venezuela) needs to buy more Primaglass resin.

Speaker A looks at this page. Speaker B turns to page 82.

SPEAKER A

Role play 2

You are Francisco Cordoves. Telephone Jim Prior. Get his advice on:
- how much resin to order
- asking for a higher discount
- delivery terms

Useful information:
You think you'll need at least 7,000 kg per month for at least six months.
You think you should ask for a discount of 8%.
You want delivery in five days.

4 Work with a partner. You are each going to prepare a short presentation.
Speaker A looks at this page. Speaker B looks at page 82.

SPEAKER A

Presentation

What is important when …?
Negotiating a deal
- getting the lowest possible price
- achieving a 'win-win' situation
- being able to cancel the deal at any time

Useful expressions:
I think that (X) is very important because …
I don't think (Y) is important because …
It's really useful to have …

Technical and social exchanges

BEFORE YOU START

1 There are two ways of describing dimensions in English. Look at the following sentences:

a) The swimming pool has *a depth of* three metres.
b) The swimming pool is three metres *deep*.

Rewrite the following description of a road.
1 Its length is 50 kilometres.
2 Its width is 10.5 metres.
3 The road surface has a thickness of five centimetres.

2 The following words in this unit may be new. Check that you understand them.
BRIEFING – an explanation given by a specialist
TRAFFIC JAM – where the road is blocked with too many vehicles
HOST – someone who invites and entertains guests

A Reading and writing

1 ◀UNIT 6▶ The Asian Investment Bank syndicate decided to send a team to Vietnam to investigate the motorway. Most of the action in this unit takes place in Hanoi (the capital).

Here is part of a letter from Le Van Nam to Dr Gerhard Leinhof, who is the Technical Director of the Bayern Bank in Munich (Germany). The bank is a member of the syndicate.

Read the letter and complete the statements on page 59.

Dear Dr Leinhof

Mr Martin Reynolds of the Asian Investment Bank in Paris has asked me to contact you directly about the technical details of the projected motorway between Hanoi and Hong Gai.

We plan a two-lane motorway of approximately 130 kilometres in length and 30 metres wide, with a six-centimetre thickness of tarmac on the road surface. About halfway along its length, we plan to modernise the connecting road to the port of Haiphong, which is to the south of Hong Gai.

Construction of the motorway is expected to take about two years and will involve the employment of both European and Vietnamese engineers. However, the workforce will be entirely Vietnamese.

Most of the heavy equipment necessary for this project is available in Vietnam, but we will probably need to transport the tarmac from near Ho Chi Minh City, in the south. We will confirm more details in the next few months.

Please let me know if you need any further information.

1 The motorway will be _____.
   a) exactly 130 kilometres long
   b) around 130 kilometres long
   c) less than 130 kilometres long

2 The motorway will be _____.
   a) 20 metres wide
   b) built with a 20-centimetre surface
   c) over 25 metres wide with a six-centimetre surface

3 There will be _____.
   a) a modernisation of Hong Gai
   b) a road linking the motorway to a port
   c) a connecting road to the south of Vietnam

4 Construction of the motorway will involve _____.
   a) Vietnamese and foreign nationals
   b) a European workforce
   c) only Vietnamese engineers

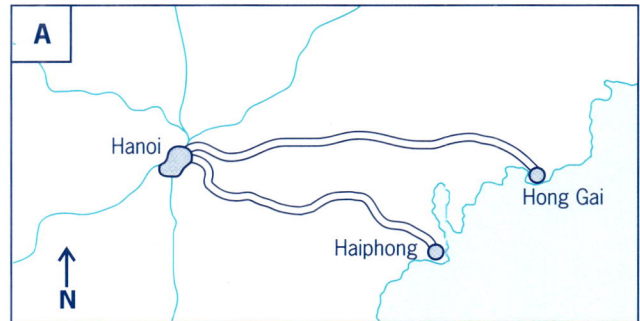

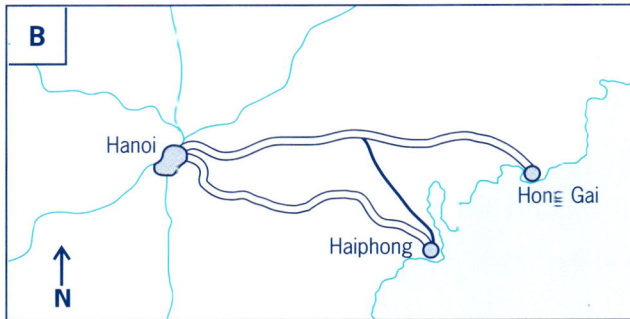

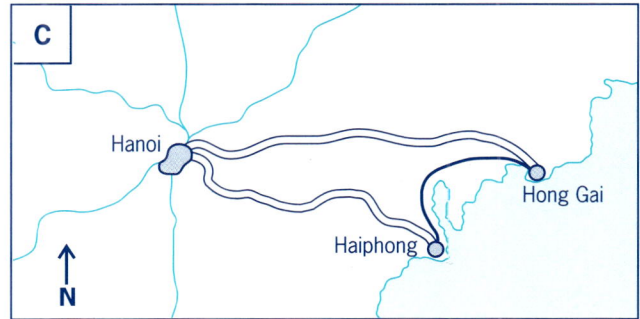

2 Look at the three motorway maps (A, B and C). Which corresponds best to the description given in Le Van Nam's letter?

3 The site visit to Vietnam was arranged for 3–4 December. In October Martin Reynolds received the following letter from Mr Nguyen Minh Tuan, First Secretary at the Ministry of Transport and Communications.

Dear Mr Reynolds

After the site visit on 4 December, we would be very pleased if you and your syndicate colleagues could join us for dinner.

I hope this date will be convenient, and look forward to meeting you all.

Yours sincerely

Nguyen Minh Tuan

Nguyen Minh Tuan
First Secretary

You are Martin Reynolds. Write a short letter of reply in which you:
• accept the invitation
• say you are looking forward to your visit

You can begin your letter like this:

Dear Mr Nguyen,

On behalf of my syndicate colleagues and myself, I would like to thank you for your kind invitation to dinner on 4 December.

Listening

1 Here is the programme that the Vietnamese Ministry of Transport and Communications arranged for the bank syndicate members.

PROGRAMME

3 December

09.00 – Welcome briefing
11.00 – Helicopter flight over Hanoi end of motorway
13.00 – Lunch
14.00 – Presentation of Hanoi end, plus questions
16.00 – Financial meetings

4 December

09.00 – Visit to Hong Gai end
12.00 – Lunch in Hong Gai
14.00 – Technical briefing, followed by return to Hanoi
19.30 – Farewell dinner

On the afternoon of 3 December, the bank syndicate members attended a presentation by Le Van Nam, the Technical Director of the Ministry of Transport and Communications.

Listen to the recording and mark the following statements true or false. Correct the sentences you think are false.

1 Many lorries were visible from the helicopter.   T   F
2 A motorway would not help traffic from the north.   T   F
3 There will be more traffic from the north in future.   T   F
4 All lorries are delayed for at least three hours.   T   F
5 Delays affect business.   T   F

2 Listen again and fill in the missing words and numbers.

1 These are mainly caused by _____ _____ of lorries that leave Hanoi every day.

2 The maximum possible speed is often only _____ _____ an hour ...

3 It's difficult to calculate, Dr Leinhof, but probably _____ _____ hours.

3 Notice how Gerhard Leinhof asked his questions. He said "Excuse me" as a way of interrupting politely. Look at the following expressions and match them with the correct situation.

1 Stop talking, please.
2 Could I just interrupt you there?
3 Just a minute.
4 Well, I'm afraid that's all we have time for today.
5 Can I come back to that later?

A You ask someone to wait on the phone while you find the person they want to speak to.
B You'd like to answer someone's question at the end of your presentation, not now.
C A parent or teacher to young children in class.
D You want to ask a question at a presentation.
E You don't want to answer any more questions.

4 🎧 During the evening of 4 December, the syndicate members and their Vietnamese hosts had dinner in a restaurant. Martin Reynolds was sitting next to Nguyen Minh Tuan.

Look at the list of eight conversation subjects below. Then listen to the conversation between Martin Reynolds and Nguyen Minh Tuan. Tick the subjects they talk about.

flying	✓	motorways	☐
trips to France	☐	finance	☐
weather	☐	French restaurants in Paris	☐
Vietnamese restaurants in Paris	☐	Vietnamese specialities	☐

5 Listen again and complete the following statements.

1 Martin Reynolds _____.
   a) enjoyed the helicopter flight
   b) thought the helicopter flight was useful
   c) likes flying

2 *Bun cha* _____.
   a) is made from beef and vegetables
   b) is difficult to cook
   c) comes from the north of the country

3 Martin Reynolds _____.
   a) has often eaten Vietnamese food before
   b) has never had Vietnamese food before
   c) has never eaten *bun cha* in Paris

4 Nguyen Minh Tuan _____.
   a) visits France on holiday
   b) visits France regularly
   c) rarely visits Parisian banks

5 At the end of their conversation _____.
   a) Martin Reynolds invites Nguyen Minh Tuan to dinner in Paris
   b) Nguyen Minh Tuan invites Martin Reynolds to dinner in Paris
   c) Martin Reynolds invites Nguyen Minh Tuan to dinner in Hanoi

6 There is one "condition" to the invitation. What is it?

6 Listen again and fill in the missing words.

1 Nguyen: *(polite enquiry)*
            _____ _____ _____ your visit?

2 Reynolds: *(response)*
            Yes, it's _____ _____ _____.

3 Reynolds: *(complimenting the host)*
            Mmm, this is _____. What's it _____?

4 Reynolds: *(complimenting the host)*
            ... but the food was _____ _____ _____ as this.

5 Reynolds: *(making an invitation)*
            ... the next time you come, you must _____ _____
            _____ you to a Vietnamese dinner.

6 Nguyen: *(accepting)*
            Thank you. It _____ _____ _____ pleasure.

1 In different cultures, different subjects are considered suitable for social conversation. In your opinion, which of the following questions are acceptable? Mark each question "A" (acceptable) or "N" (not acceptable) in your country.

1	Are you religious?	A	N
2	Do you have a family?	A	N
3	How old are you?	A	N
4	How much money do you earn?	A	N
5	Do you travel much in your job?	A	N
6	Which political party do you support?	A	N
7	Where do you spend your holidays?	A	N
8	Do you like your job?	A	N
9	Do you go to the theatre much?	A	N
10	Do you prefer working with men or women?	A	N

Now check your answers with a partner. Do you agree?

2 Match the invitations (1–6) with the replies (A–F).

1 What about lunch tomorrow? Are you free?

2 Would you like to visit the Arts Museum this afternoon?

3 Why not come round later for drinks?

4 How about going to a night club on Saturday?

5 Can I give you a lift?

6 Would you like a beer?

A OK, what time?

B Thanks, but I'd prefer a soft drink.

C Sorry, but I never eat at midday.

D Great! Which one?

E No, it's OK. I'll get a taxi.

F I'd love to. Are there any famous pictures there?

3 Role plays 1, 2 and 3 are all for two students.

It is 4 December. The dinner in the Vietnamese restaurant is just ending. The bank syndicate members will fly back to Paris the following day, 5 December, in the evening.

Speaker A looks at this page. Speaker B turns to page 82.

Speaker B turns to page 82.

SPEAKER A

Role play 1

You are a Vietnamese official.
• Invite your partner (a bank syndicate member) and his/her colleagues to visit a famous temple with you tomorrow morning.

Additional information:
meet at hotel / 9 am
drive to the temple to arrive / 11 am
walk around temple and gardens / see wonderful view
have lunch / famous local restaurant
return to hotel / 4.30 pm
book taxi to airport

Role play 2

You are a Vietnamese official.
• Invite your partner (a bank syndicate member) to a nearby night club that you know.
• Respond to the request that your partner then makes and offer to accompany him/her.
• Agree a time and place to meet.

Additional information:
There's a good choice of gifts in the local market.
The market is open from 10 am.

Role play 3

You are a bank syndicate member. Your partner (a Vietnamese official) is coming to Paris next month.
• Ask when he/she is travelling.
• Invite him/her to dinner in Paris.
• Give him/her your telephone number and ask him/her to contact you.
• Ask him/her what kind of food he/she likes.

UNIT 11

Enquiries and complaints

1 Read the following dialogue, then make Speaker A's enquiries more polite by using the forms in the box below.

A: When does the drinks party start?
B: At 6.30 pm.
A: Where?
B: In the exhibition room.

A: Will it last long?
B: About an hour, I think.
A: What about food?
B: There'll be snacks, of course.
A: OK.

Can you tell me ...?	And will there be any ...?
How long ... please?	Thank you. And where ... be?

2 The following words in this unit may be new. Check that you understand them.

AUDITORIUM – a large room used for conference lectures
BANQUET – a large formal dinner
PLENARY LECTURE – a speech by a well-known specialist
POSTER EXHIBITION – an exhibition of work-in-progress
PANEL DISCUSSION – a group of experts discuss a subject
EVENING DRESS – smart clothes for a formal occasion

A Reading and writing

1 ◀ UNIT 7 ▶ Two weeks before the conference began, everybody at Research Exchange was very busy. Here is the first day of the conference programme.

GENETIC CAUSES OF HEART DISEASE
CONFERENCE PROGRAMME

28 October

09.00	Welcome speech (auditorium). Professor Anna Jager (Amsterdam State University, Netherlands)
09.30	Plenary lecture (auditorium). "Heart disease – the limits of genetics". Dr Albert Jameson (Washington State Hospital, USA)
10.30	Coffee and poster exhibition
11.30–12.00	"Genetic Defects in Athletes" (room 103). Dr Isabelle Carrier (Cardiac Research Institute, Paris, France)
12.00–12.30	"Genetics and populations" (room 105). Dr Margaret Boka (University Hospital, Harare, Zimbabwe)
12.30–14.00	Lunch
14.30–15.30	Panel discussion (auditorium). "Fighting Heart Disease", with Professor Anna Jager, Professor Johannes Klein and Dr Albert Jameson
15.30	Coffee and poster exhibition
17.00–17.30	"Beyond beta-blockers" (room 107). Dr Marie-Laure Foucault (Pharmasynthesis, Berne, Switzerland)
17.30–18.00	"Family genetic groups – a Russian experiment" (room 105). Dr Anya Nabokova (Moscow Medical School, Moscow, Russia)
18.30	Drinks party
20.00	Dinner

Refer to the conference programme and complete the following summary.

The conference will be opened by Professor Anna Jager of
(1) _Amsterdam State University_, and she will be followed by Dr Albert
Jameson, who will give the (2) _____. At the coffee break,
participants will be able to walk around the (3) _____ and discuss
current research work with their colleagues. The two final presentations of
the morning will be by (4) _____ and (5) _____, from
France and (6) _____ respectively.

  After lunch there will be a panel discussion with three well-known
specialists. This will last for (7) _____, and will be followed by a
second opportunity to discuss work-in-progress which will begin at
(8) _____. Two more presentations will conclude the afternoon,
after which we shall hold a (9) _____: all participants and their
partners are invited. Finally, dinner will be served at (10) _____.

2   Refer to the conference programme again and write answers to the following
    questions.

    1 Where does the plenary lecture take place? _In the auditorium_ _____

    2 What date does the conference begin? _____

    3 What time is the first coffee break? _____

    4 What time is lunch? _____

    5 When does Dr Boka's presentation start? _____

    6 Where is Dr Foucault's presentation? _____

    7 Which two presentations will take place in the same room? _____

       _____

    8 What time is the drinks party? _____

3   Before the conference Ellen Bakker received this e-mail from
    Pharmasynthesis. It contains some errors. Mark the errors and then write out
    a correct version of the e-mail.

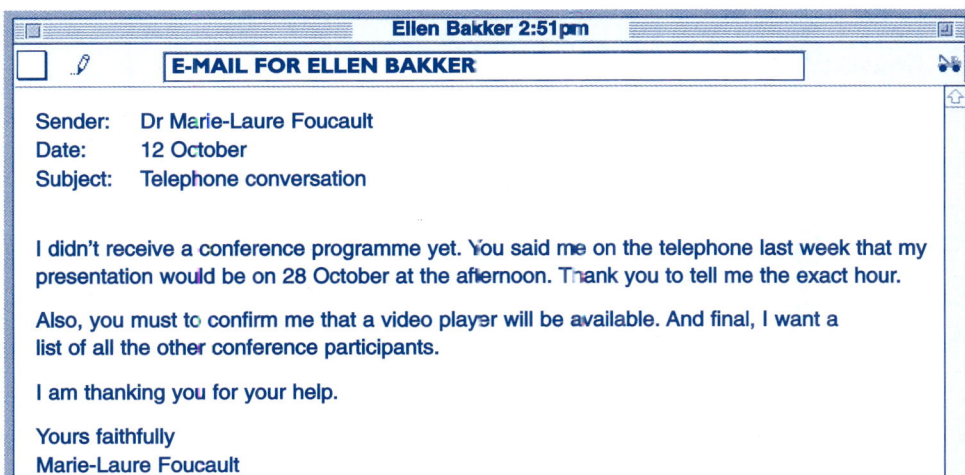

```
┌──────────────────────────────────────────────────────────────────────┐
│ ▦▦              Ellen Bakker 2:51pm                                ▦   │
├──────────────────────────────────────────────────────────────────────┤
│ ☐  ✎   E-MAIL FOR ELLEN BAKKER                                     ⋈   │
├──────────────────────────────────────────────────────────────────────┤
│                                                                     ⇧  │
│  Sender:   Dr Marie-Laure Foucault                                     │
│  Date:     12 October                                                  │
│  Subject:  Telephone conversation                                      │
│                                                                        │
│  I didn't receive a conference programme yet. You said me on the       │
│  telephone last week that my presentation would be on 28 October at    │
│  the afternoon. Thank you to tell me the exact hour.                    │
│                                                                        │
│  Also, you must to confirm me that a video player will be available.   │
│  And final, I want a list of all the other conference participants.    │
│                                                                        │
│  I am thanking you for your help.                                      │
│                                                                        │
│  Yours faithfully                                                      │
│  Marie-Laure Foucault                                                  │
└──────────────────────────────────────────────────────────────────────┘
```

4   Refer to the conference programme and write a reply to Dr Foucault's e-mail.

Listening

1 During the conference Wim Lubbers was very busy. First look at the social programme he organised for the partners of people attending the conference.

SOCIAL PROGRAMME AND TRIPS
....

28 October
18.30 – Drinks party

29 October
Full-day trip to Amsterdam. Departure by coach at 09.00 from the Utrecht Conference Centre. In the morning we will visit the Rijksmuseum, Amsterdam's most famous art gallery. An English-speaking guide will accompany our party. In the afternoon you will have a chance to explore the "Old Town" or visit the shops. The coach back to Utrecht will leave at 17.00.

Price: 55 euros

30 October
A morning in Amsterdam (the "Venice of the North"). Departure by coach at 09.00 from the Utrecht Conference Centre. We will go on a boat trip along the city's beautiful canals with an English-speaking guide. This will be followed by lunch at a well-known waterside restaurant. The coach back to Utrecht will leave at 15.00.

Price: 65 euros (includes lunch)

20.30 – Banquet at the Excelsior Hotel, Utrecht. Evening dress.

🎧 During the conference, Wim Lubbers was asked several questions about the social programme. You will hear four short conversations. Refer to the social programme and complete the exercises that follow.

1 There are two questions for Wim Lubbers. The first is about the

_____ of the cocktail party.
a) time   b) duration   c) place

2 The second question is about _____.
a) drinks   b) speeches   c) clothes

2 Now listen again and fill in the missing words.

1 _____ _____, about the drinks party this evening. How long

_____ ____ _____?

2 OK. Oh, and _____ _____. Is it formal? _____ _____, evening dress?

3 🎧 Listen to the recording and mark these statements true or false. Correct the sentences you think are false.

1 The questioner wants to visit the Rijksmuseum.   T   F
2 The questioner doesn't speak English.   T   F
3 The questioner's wife speaks French.   T   F
4 No French-speaking guides are needed.   T   F
5 Wim Lubbers will contact the Rijksmuseum.   T   F

4 Listen again to how the questioner makes his enquiries. What does he say?

1 I _____ ____ _____, Mr Lubbers.

2 Well, _____ _____ _____, my wife's English is not very good.

3 Do _____ _____ _____ the guide speaks French?

5 🎧 Listen to someone making a complaint to Wim Lubbers, and complete the following statements.

1 Why is the person complaining? Because _____.
   a) it was raining in Amsterdam
   b) her husband drank wine
   c) her husband had to pay for wine

2 She thought that _____.
   a) wine was provided with lunch
   b) fifteen euros was not expensive
   c) the social programme was very good

6 Listen again to how the questioner makes her complaint and how Wim Lubbers answers her. Then fill in the missing words.

1 Lubbers: Oh, what _____ _____.

2 Woman: But that's _____ _____ _____, Mr Lubbers.

3 Woman: Look, on the programme it says that lunch is included,

          _____?

4 Lubbers: I'm _____ _____ _____. But you see, wine
           wasn't included in the price.

7 🎧 Listen to the next question that Wim Lubbers is asked, then mark these statements true or false. Correct the sentences you think are false.

1 The questioner wants to know about _____.
   a) the banquet
   b) special menus
   c) her application form

2 Wim Lubbers says he _____.
   a) will look for the application form
   b) likes vegetarian food
   c) will deal with the problem

8 Listen again to how the questioner makes her enquiry and how Wim Lubbers responds. Fill in the missing words.

1 Woman: Could _____ _____ _____ if there are vegetarian
          menus ...?

2 Lubbers: Did _____ _____ _____ one on your application form?

3 Woman: I'm _____ _____. I forgot.

4 Lubbers: Don't _____. I'll _____ _____ _____.

C Speaking

1 During the conference, all the employees of Research Exchange were present. They had to answer a lot of enquiries and deal with problems.

Here are some of the questions people asked them. Who probably dealt with the following enquiries?

- Ellen Bakker (EB) – Organisation Manager
- Wim Lubbers (WL) – Social and Leisure Manager
- Jennie Carpenter (JC) – Secretary and Accommodation Manager

Tick the correct column after each question.

	EB	WL	JC
1 My bedroom's noisy. Is it possible to change?	____	____	____
2 Do you know a good restaurant in Amsterdam?	____	____	____
3 Does the canal guide speak German?	____	____	____
4 Does my room have a video screen?	____	____	____
5 How long will Dr Matsuhito's presentation last?	____	____	____
6 Could you help me? I've lost my room key.	____	____	____

2 Now match the following answers with the questions above.

	Question
a) I think he does, yes.	_3_
b) Thirty minutes.	____
c) Oh, dear. When did you last see it?	____
d) It's not easy. Which hotel are you in?	____
e) I'd try the Reefer.	____
f) I'm not sure. Did you ask for one?	____

3 Complete the following conversation between Jennie Carpenter and a conference participant. Use the information below.

1 Participant: Can you tell me _when Dr Carrier's presentation is, please_ ?

2 Carpenter: Certainly. _____.

3 Participant: And do you know _____?

4 Carpenter: About _____.

5 Participant: And _____?

6 Carpenter: At 12.30.

7 Participant: Thank you.

8 Carpenter: You're welcome.

at / 103 / room / 11.30 / in
an / half / hour
~~is / please / Dr Carrier's / when / presentation~~
time / what / is / lunch
will / last / long / it / how

4 Role plays 1 and 2 are both for two students.

One of you is a participant in the Utrecht conference, and the other is a Research Exchange employee.

Speaker A looks at this page. Speaker B turns to page 83.

SPEAKER A

Role play 1

You are Dr Yukio Matsuhito, from Japan. You are speaking to Ellen Bakker. You want to know:
- why Dr Richardson cannot speak at the plenary session on 30 October
- who the new speaker at the plenary session on 30 October is
- what the new speaker will talk about

Useful questions and expressions:
Could you tell me who ...?
What is the subject of ...?

Role play 2

You are Dr Margaret Boka, from Zimbabwe. You are speaking to Jennie Carpenter. You are staying at the Centraal Hotel. You are on the first floor of the hotel and your room faces the street. It is very noisy and you cannot sleep at night.
- Ask Jennie Carpenter to help you change rooms.

Useful questions and expressions:
Could I have a word with you?
I'm afraid there's a problem with ...

5 Work with a partner. You are each going to prepare a short presentation.
Speaker A looks at this page. Speaker B looks at page 83.

SPEAKER A

Presentation

What is important when ...?
Asking for information in English
- perfect grammar
- good pronunciation
- a pen to note down information

Useful expressions:
I think that (X) is very important because ...
I don't think (Y) is important because ...
It's really useful to have...

Tasks and teams

setting tasks

organising teams

defining responsibilities

working to deadlines

BEFORE YOU START

1 Complete the following sentences using the words in the box.

reports	look	responsible	in charge	down

1 Ilona Tolnai is _____ of distribution.

2 Nicci Garland _____ to Charlie Jennings.

3 It's _____ to Tom if the project doesn't succeed.

4 Magyar Ventures will _____ after central European sales.

5 Macro Music is _____ for The Trainspotters.

2 The following words in this unit may be new. Check you understand them.
PUBLICIST – someone who works in publicity or advertising
HALL – (here) a place where concerts take place
CLIENT RECORDS – written details of clients
TO INTERPRET – to translate orally between languages

A Reading and writing

1 ◀ UNIT 8 ▶ It was time for The Trainspotters' European tour. Macro Music was responsible for the western European countries while the central European part of the tour was organised by Magyar Ventures.

To help Magyar Ventures with the tour organisation, Tom Masters sent his assistant, Bill Palmer, to Budapest for three months. Bill was an experienced publicist, and arranged for Ilona Tolnai to be interviewed in an English-language Budapest newspaper.

Read the extract from the interview, then answer the questions.

Q What's it like working with Macro Music?

IT Very exciting. We have several projects with them. First, websites. We have a lot of technical experience in this area, so we're extending into the direct downloading of music. Then there's distribution. We already distribute computer equipment and by the end of the year we'll be arranging all Macro Music's distribution in central Europe.

Q I heard you were moving into the concert business. Is that true?

IT In a way, yes. We'll look after the practical aspects of performances in central Europe, in collaboration with Macro Music, of course.

Q What will this involve?

IT Well, apart from our Internet activities, we'll take care of advertising and ticket sales. That's the main job. But we'll also be responsible for travel and accommodation arrangements.

Q That's a new departure for Magyar Ventures, isn't it?

IT Yes, and it's certainly a challenge. But Bill Palmer has come over from Macro Music in London to help us get started.

Q And what's the first project?

IT A very exciting one. You know the British group The Trainspotters? Well, they're coming on their first European tour next month. And Magyar Ventures will arrange all their central European concerts. I've listened to their music, and it's great. We're going to have a big success!

Q Well, I wish you luck.

IT Thank you.

1 What does Ilona Tolnai think of Macro Music?
2 She has several projects with Macro Music. What are they?
3 Where will Magyar Ventures operate?
4 What will its responsibilities be?
5 Has Magyar Ventures looked after performances before?
6 How will Macro Music help Magyar Ventures?
7 When will The Trainspotters come to Budapest?
8 What does Ilona Tolnai think of The Trainspotters?

2 The Trainspotters' concert in Budapest was booked to take place the
following month. Ilona Tolnai worked closely with Bill Palmer and also with
her assistant, Marianna Koloti. There was still a lot to do.
    Ilona wrote a chart to show the different tasks. She put initials next to each
task to show who was responsible for it: IT – Ilona Tolnai, BP – Bill Palmer or
MK – Marianna Koloti.

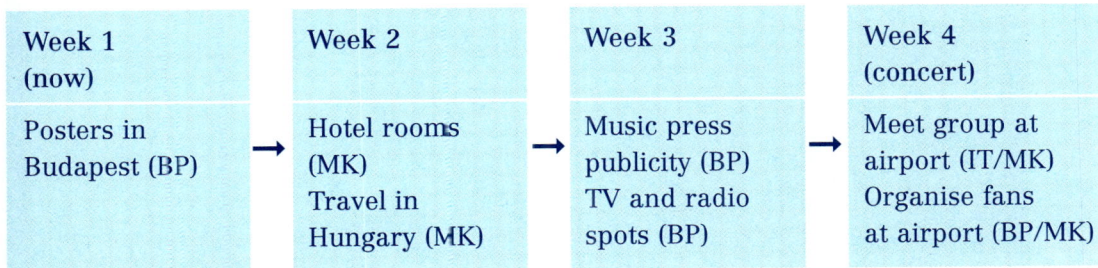

Week 1 (now)	Week 2	Week 3	Week 4 (concert)
Posters in Budapest (BP)	Hotel rooms (MK) Travel in Hungary (MK)	Music press publicity (BP) TV and radio spots (BP)	Meet group at airport (IT/MK) Organise fans at airport (BP/MK)

Ilona Tolnai sent a copy of
the chart to Tom Masters,
along with a fax about the
responsibilities of the team
and the deadlines for the
tasks.
    Complete the fax using
the words in the box.

at the latest
deal with
report
in charge
responsible
to look after
by

Dear Tom

Everything is going well here, and the preparations for the tour
are nearly ready. Bill has been a great help! Now, looking at
the chart:

Week 1: As you can see, I have asked Bill (1) _____
the posters in Budapest and they look very attractive. The first
ones will be displayed by the end of this week (2) _____.

Week 2: Marianna Koloti will (3) _____ hotel and travel
arrangements, and will (4) _____ directly to me.

Week 3: (5) _____ this time, the publicity spots will be
organised. Bill is (6) _____ of this.

Week 4: The big day will be on Friday, when Marianna and I will
meet The Trainspotters at Budapest airport. Marianna and Bill will
be (7) _____ for the welcome by the fans.

Let me know if this is OK.

All the best,
Ilona

1 🎧 The Trainspotters' concert in Budapest was to be held on Friday 13 November. On Monday 9 Tom Masters telephoned Ilona Tolnai to tell her about a problem and to check final arrangements. Their conversation is in four parts. Listen to all the parts, then complete the following statements.

1 In the first part of the conversation they discuss _____.
   a) Alex, the singer in the band
   b) one of the musicians in the band
   c) different hospitals

2 Then they talk about _____.
   a) future concerts
   b) Budapest
   c) accommodation

3 In the third part they discuss _____.
   a) Marianna's capabilities
   b) Marianna's language
   c) another assistant

4 And finally Ilona Tolnai mentions _____.
   a) a thousand tickets
   b) a concert on Thursday
   c) a delivery of CDs

2 Listen again and answer the following questions.

Part 1
1 What has happened to the saxophone player?
2 What must Tom Masters do quickly?

Part 2
3 Is the Hungarian public interested in The Trainspotters?

4 One of Marianna Koloti's responsibilities is to _____ _____ the hotel booking.

Part 3
5 What does Tom Masters want to do about interpreting?

6 Ilona Tolnai doesn't agree. She says she is sure that Marianna will _____

_____ the interpreting very well.

7 Ilona Tolnai says professional interpreters are _____.
a) incapable   b) a good idea   c) expensive

Part 4
8 What's the problem with the CDs?
9 Ilona Tolnai needs them by Thursday _____ _____ _____.

3 🎧 On 19 November Tom Masters went to Budapest to discuss co-operation between Magyar Ventures and Macro Music. During the meeting at Magyar Ventures, Ilona Tolnai gave a short presentation about future developments in Hungary. Bill Palmer was also present.
Listen to the recording and then mark these statements true or false. Correct the sentences you think are false.

1 Ilona Tolnai's presentation will be about finance.	T	F
2 She wants English people to process CD orders.	T	F
3 Magyar Ventures possesses good storage facilities.	T	F
4 The Accounts Department at Magyar Ventures needs extra staff.	T	F
5 Macro Music will be responsible for transport.	T	F

4 Listen again and fill in the missing words.

1 Tolnai: To begin with, we must _____ a _____ to process telephone orders ...

2 Tolnai: I suggest a small team _____ _____ an English-speaking person.

3 Tolnai: We already have a very efficient warehouse thirty kilometres from Budapest, but it'll _____ some _____. I'll _____ _____ that.

4 Masters: Won't you need a separate team _____ _____ _____ ?

Speaking

1 Look at the organisation chart. Then complete the sentences below, using the words in the box.

```
┌─────────────────────────┐
│   Managing Director      │
│   Tim Harris             │
└─────────────────────────┘
            │
┌─────────────────────────┐
│ Sales and Marketing Director │
│ Cathy McCabe             │
└─────────────────────────┘
            │
┌─────────────────────────┐
│ Sales Manager (UK and Europe) │
│ Mark Watson              │
└─────────────────────────┘
            │
┌─────────────────────────┐
│ Senior Sales Supervisor  │
│ Maria Roselli            │
└─────────────────────────┘
            │
     ┌──────┴──────┐
┌──────────────┐  ┌──────────────────┐
│ Sales Executive (UK) │  │ Sales Executive (Europe) │
│ Sally Boyd   │  │ Jacques Laude    │
└──────────────┘  └──────────────────┘
```

manages	deals with	responsibility	reports to	supervises

1 Cathy McCabe _____ the Managing Director.

2 Maria Roselli _____ the Sales Executives.

3 Mark Watson _____ the Sales Department.

4 Jacques Laude _____ European sales.

5 UK sales are Sally Boyd's _____ .

2 Match the phrases below to make complete sentences.

1 Our objectives	A co-ordinate our strategy.
2 Designing an attractive	B be in charge of payments?
3 The main objectives are	C to look after distribution.
4 Shouldn't Magyar Ventures	D must be defined properly.
5 I suggest that	E efficiency and good service.
6 It's vital that we	F with special orders?
7 He's the best person	G Macro Music handles publicity.
8 How should we deal	H website is our first aim.

3 Role play 1 is for two speakers.

After Ilona Tolnai had finished her presentation, she and Tom Masters discussed future collaboration between Macro Music and Magyar Ventures.

Speaker A looks at this page. Speaker B turns to page 83.

SPEAKER A

Role play 1

You are Tom Masters. You want:
- greater control for Macro Music of operations and costs
- Magyar Ventures to be responsible for distribution throughout central Europe
- Magyar Ventures to be responsible for all advertising and publicity costs
- ten major European music tours per year
- Magyar to use an agency to book hotels and travel for tours

Try to define common objectives and come to an agreement about reponsibilities.

Role play 2 is for two speakers.

ILTEC is a company that has organisational problems. The Managing Director has called a meeting with the Marketing Manager to discuss these.

Speaker A looks at this page. Speaker B turns to page 83.

SPEAKER A

Role play 2

ILTEC employs 35 sales people who report individually to the Marketing Manager. Distribution takes place from a large central warehouse. At present the system is very inefficient. For instance:
- the Marketing Manager has too much work
- liaison between the sales staff and the warehouse is bad
- distribution is inefficient
- orders are often delivered late

You are the Managing Director. You want to reorganise the sales department as follows:
- three regional warehouses
- a senior sales supervisor to be responsible for each warehouse and region
- each supervisor to report to the Marketing Manager
- twelve sales people per region, responsible to the senior sales supervisors

Discuss how the present distribution system can be improved. Try to come to an agreement. Then draw an organisation chart of the new tasks and responsibilities.

Role Play: Speaker B/C

UNIT 1

SPEAKER B

Role play 1

You are Pablo Torres. Manuel Ortega (Speaker A) will introduce you to Michelle Henderson (Speaker C).
- Greet Michelle Henderson and ask when she arrived in Caracas.
- Ask about her hotel and her first impressions of the city.
- Then answer her questions.

Useful questions:
When did you ...?
What's your hotel like? Is it comfortable?
What do you think of Caracas?

Useful information:
You love sailing and you go sailing at weekends.
You have your own boat.

Role play 2

You are Jim Prior.
- Answer Pablo Torres (Speaker A)'s questions about Florida Marine.

Useful information:
Your company is based in Miami.
You produce sailing boats.
Your market share is around 20%.
There is limited expansion in the States.

Role play 3

You are Pablo Torres.
- Answer Jim Prior (Speaker A)'s questions.

Useful information:
You live 30 km from Caracas, near the sea.
You are a company lawyer for a German multinational.
You often travel to Hamburg on business.

UNIT 2

Speaker B   Pair work

Dictate the following sentences to your partner.

1 The flight arrives at 17.15.

2 The flight number is BA 7083.

3 A return ticket costs 745 euros.

4 The flight is delayed by 45 minutes.

5 The check-in time is 4 o'clock.

Now listen to Speaker A and note down the information.

1 Take-off time: _____

2 Cost of ticket: _____

3 Original arrival time of flight: _____

4 Flight number: _____

5 Check-in time: _____

UNIT 2
SPEAKER B

Role play 1

You work in the reservations department of Air France. You will receive a telephone call.
- Get the name and flight date of your caller and make his reservation (there are seats).
- Then refer to the timetable to answer his questions.

Flight	Paris	Hanoi (local time)	Days
AF 172	19.40	15.25 (next day)	Tues/Fri
AF 174	21.30	17.40 (next day)	Sun/Thur

Duration: 14.5 hours
Stopover: Bangkok (1.5 hours)
Facilities: 2 films – dinner – light lunch

Role play 2

You are Jim McBride. You work in Edinburgh. Sylvie Lavigne is a friend. She sends you this e-mail:

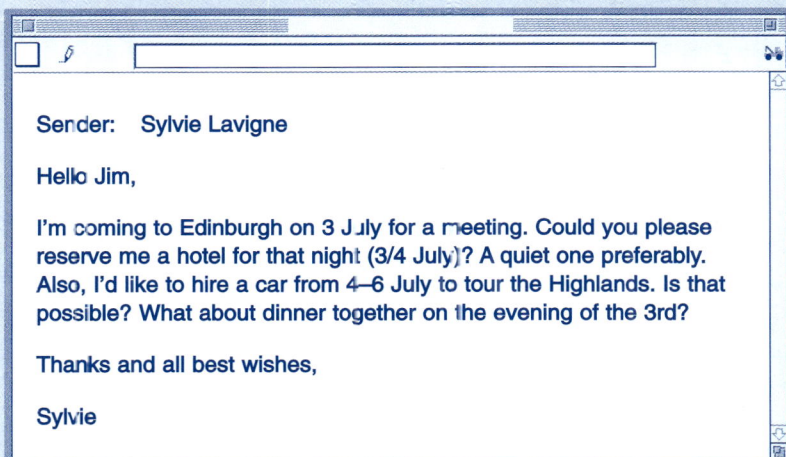

Sender: Sylvie Lavigne

Hello Jim,

I'm coming to Edinburgh on 3 July for a meeting. Could you please reserve me a hotel for that night (3/4 July)? A quiet one preferably. Also, I'd like to hire a car from 4–6 July to tour the Highlands. Is that possible? What about dinner together on the evening of the 3rd?

Thanks and all best wishes,

Sylvie

- Now telephone Sylvie Lavigne and give her your information.
- Accept her invitation to dinner on 3 July.

Useful information:
You've booked a single room at the Glencoe Hotel (quiet part of Edinburgh).
Car hire no problem (need French licence).

Presentation

What is important when …?
Going on a business trip
- a really good seat on the plane
- clothes to suit the climate
- an excellent hotel to stay in

Useful expressions:
I think that (X) is very important because …
I don't think (Y) is important because …
It's really useful to have …

Role play 1

You are Dr Isabelle Carrier of the Cardiac Research Institute in Paris (France). You will receive a telephone call from Ellen Bakker.
• Answer her query.

Useful information:
The title of your presentation is "Genetic Defects in Athletes".

Role play 2

You are Ellen Bakker. One of the conference participants will telephone you with a problem.
• Get his name and details, and then try to help him.

Useful information:
It is possible to change the time of his presentation to 29 October at 2 o'clock in the afternoon.

Role play 3

You are the secretary of Dr Li Yang of Number 2 Hospital in Beijing (China). You receive an urgent call for him.
• Take a message.

Useful information:
Dr Li is in America this week, but he will return to Beijing next Monday.

Role play 4

You are Jennie Carpenter. You will receive a call for Ellen Bakker from a participant in the conference. Ellen is at lunch.
• Get the caller's name and details, and then take a message for Ellen.

Role play 1

You are Nicci Garland. You would prefer to work with a British website design company. In your opinion:
• Communications would be much easier.
• Magyar Ventures does not have enough experience.
Also, your brother manages a website marketing company in London.
Discuss your views with Tom Masters.

Role play 2

You will discuss the possibility of Macro Music organising a "political" rock concert.
   You are Charlie Jennings. Your partner (Nicci Garland) will begin the conversation. You do not agree with her idea.
• You do not want to confuse music and politics.
• The idea is financially risky.
• Well-known musicians would want payment.
• It would be bad for sales in certain countries.

Presentation

What is important when …?
Working with a foreign company
• good communications
• having exactly the same work methods
• knowing a lot about the company

Useful expressions:
I think that (X) is very important because …
I don't think (Y) is important because …
It's really useful to have …

UNIT 5
SPEAKER B

In each of these role plays, Speaker A will ask you for something. Look at the notice and then reply, making a suggestion.

Role play 1

Notice: COCKTAIL BAR OPEN 6–10 pm
EVERY WEEKDAY EVENING

Suggestion: wait for half an hour

Role play 2

Notice: A HOTEL BUS LEAVES FOR THE TOWN CENTRE EVERY HOUR ON THE HOUR

Suggestion: take a taxi

Role play 3

Notice: ROOM SERVICE MEALS AVAILABLE UNTIL 9.00 pm

Suggestion: pizza restaurant near hotel

Role play 4

You are a visitor to Florida Marine. Your partner will describe the layout of their offices and what is done in each department. Ask for repetition and clarification if necessary, and fill in the plan on the right.

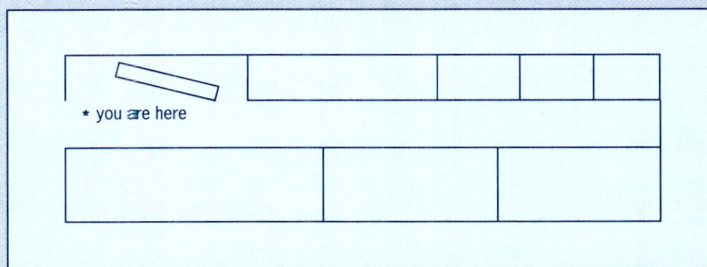

* you are here

UNIT 6
Speaker B   Pair work

Your partner will describe a graph showing Japanese investment in Vietnam. Fill in the details below and complete the graph on the right.

Year   Figure

_____ _____

_____ _____

_____ _____

1992   1993   1998

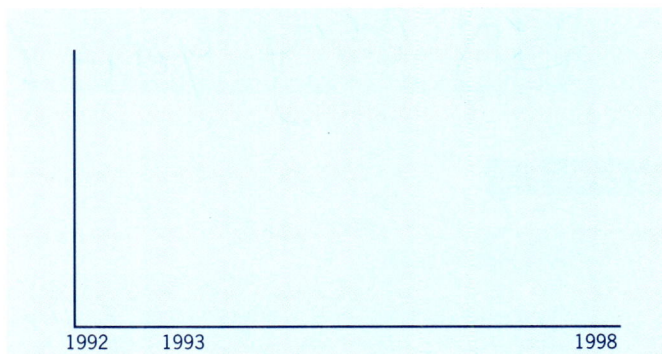

Now look at this graph showing Vietnam's industrial growth (in percentage terms) between 1991 and 1998. Describe it to your partner.

1991	10.4%
1995	14.5%
1998	12.1%

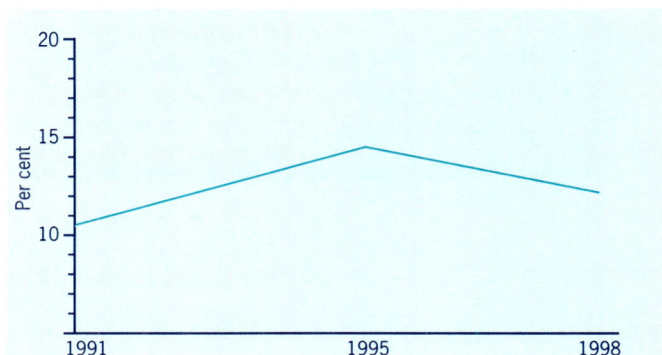

Per cent

1991   1995   1998

UNIT 1

Role play 1

You are Michelle Henderson. Manuel Ortega (Speaker A) will introduce you to Pablo Torres (Speaker B).

- Greet Pablo Torres and answer his questions.
- Then ask him about sailing.

Useful information:
You have been in Caracas for three days.
You are staying at the luxurious Grandioso Hotel.
You have not had time for tourism.

Useful questions:
Do you like sailing?
How often do you sail?
Do you have your own boat?

UNIT 6

Role play 1

You organise coach tours in Europe. You specialise in tours for senior citizens, and you want to find out about the long-term possibilities of the Japanese market. In particular, you want to know about the demographic "profile" of Japan. Speaker A is an expert on Japan.

- Introduce yourself (use your real name).
- Tell Speaker A what you hope to do.
- Ask him/her to tell you about demographic trends.

Role play 2

You are the publisher of a business women's magazine, *Woman Executive*, which is successful in many countries. You want to find out about the possibility of launching a Japanese language version. For this, you need to know more about the position of Japanese women at work, and in particular, those in management positions. Speaker A is an expert on Japan.

- Introduce yourself (use your real name).
- Tell Speaker A what you hope to do.
- Ask him/her to tell you about trends in women's employment.

UNIT 7
SPEAKER B

Role play 1

You are a government official in Bratislava. The Investment Manager of Karnak Stores has come to make a presentation. Makes notes during his/her presentation. After the presentation, you want to know:
- the qualifications necessary for Slovak employees (languages? management qualifications?)
- where Karnak Stores wants to open its new store
- when Karnak Stores hopes to open

Role play 2

You are an executive from Zahn Technik. Make notes during the presentation by the Director of the Utrecht Conference Centre. After the presentation, you want to know:
- what communication facilities are available
- the size of the meeting rooms
- if there are bedrooms at the Centre

UNIT 8
SPEAKER B

Role play 1

You are Gustav Richter. During your meeting note down what you agree.
You want:
- non-American film music (too much competition from other orchestras)
- the recordings to be next August; concerts planned in May/June (musicians on holiday in July – need to change holiday dates?)
- the advertising budget to be 20% Wienbad Youth Orchestra and 80% Macro Music (refer to Tom Masters's letter of 29 October)
- non-commercial sponsorship (eg from Wienbad Arts Council)

Write a letter to Tom Masters confirming the terms of your agreement.

Role play 2

You are Tom Masters.
- Agree with Charlie Jennings how Macro Music's costs can be cut.
  Here is a breakdown of current costs, which add up to £450,000 a year.

Staff costs (salaries)	% of total costs	Other costs	
Directors (3)	25%	Studios	10%
Administrative staff (4)	15%	Advertising	20%
Drivers (2)	10%	Travel & accommodation	10%
Publicist (1)	5%	General	3%
Trainee (1)	2%		

SPEAKER B

Role play 1

You are Manuel Ortega. Jim Prior will telephone you.
- Find out what Jim Prior's offer is.
- Discuss prices and conditions. You want the following conditions:
  - discount: 5%
  - if they order more than 3,000 kg a month, extra discount of 2%
  - delivery in four days
- Note down what you agree.

Florida Marine will order:

_____ kg of _____ per _____ for a _____

Base price: $190 per 100 kg   Discount: _____%

If they order more than 3,000 kg a month, extra discount of _____%   Delivery in _____ days

- Now write a fax from Manuel Ortega to Jim Prior, confirming what you have agreed.

Role play 2

You are Jim Prior. Francisco Cordoves will call and ask you for advice.

- Ask him how much resin he'll need, and for how long. (Answer: _____)
- Ask him what discount and delivery terms he'd like to agree.
  (Answer: _____)
- Instruct him to ask for a 12% discount for the next six months.
- If Ortega doesn't agree, Cordoves should accept an 8% discount for twelve months.

Presentation

What is important when …?
Deciding how to transport goods
- reliability and safety
- speed of delivery
- cost

Useful expressions:
I think that (X) is very important because …
I don't think (Y) is important because …
It's really useful to have …

SPEAKER B

Role play 1

You are a bank syndicate member. You will receive an invitation from a Vietnamese official.
- Accept the invitation with thanks.
- Ask him/her about arrangements for the day, and make a note of them.
You need to be at the airport to check in by 8 pm.

Role play 2

You are a bank syndicate member. You will receive an invitation from a Vietnamese official.
- Refuse the invitation, with thanks. (You are very tired this evening.)
- Ask for advice about buying gifts to take home.
- Accept his/her invitation for tomorrow.
- Ask him/her about arrangements.

Role play 3

You are a Vietnamese official. You are planning to visit Paris next month. Your partner (a bank syndicate member) will ask you some questions and make an invitation.
- Accept the invitation you receive, with thanks.

Additional information:
You are travelling on 19th next month.
You like Chinese and Indian food very much.

UNIT 11
SPEAKER B

Role play 1

You are Ellen Bakker. Dr Matsuhito will ask you about a change in the conference programme.
• Answer Dr Matsuhito's queries.

Useful information:
Dr Richardson cannot speak at the plenary session on 30 October. He is ill.
His place will be taken by Dr Escobar from Portugal.
Dr Escobar will speak about heart disease and food.

Useful expressions:
I'm sorry, but …   His subject will be …

Role play 2

You are Jennie Carpenter. Dr Boka from Zimbabwe will make a complaint.
• Respond to her complaint.

Useful information:
There are no other rooms available at the Centraal Hotel.
The Excelsior Hotel is in a quiet area, but it's very expensive.
One of the conference participants is unwell, and has gone home. He was staying at the Park Hotel, 15 km outside Utrecht. Maybe his room is still free.

Presentation

What is important when …?
Attending a conference
• good organisation
• good food and wine
• interesting speakers

Useful expressions:
I think that (X) is very important because …
I don't think (Y) is important because …
It's really useful to have …

UNIT 12
SPEAKER B

Role play 1

You are Ilona Tolnai. You want:
• control of operations and costs in Hungary (your responsibility)
• responsibility for Hungarian distribution only
• to share the costs of advertising and publicity with Macro Music
• a maximum of five music tours a year
• Marianna Koloti to be responsible for hotel bookings and travel organisation

Try to define common objectives and come to an agreement about reponsibilities.

Role play 2

ILTEC employs 35 sales people who report individually to the Marketing Manager. Distribution takes place from a large central warehouse. At present the system is very inefficient. For instance:
• the Marketing Manager has too much work
• liaison between the sales staff and the warehouse is bad
• distribution is inefficient
• orders are often delivered late

You are the Marketing Manager. You want:
• to keep the central warehouse
• a new assistant to be responsible for relations with the sales people
• a new Distribution Manager to work in the warehouse
• more administrative staff in the warehouse

Discuss how the present distribution system can be improved. Try to come to an agreement. Then draw an organisation chart of the new tasks and responsibilities.

Tapescript

UNIT 1 Part B

Exercises 2 and 3

> MO = Manuel Ortega
> JP = Jim Prior
> MH = Michelle Henderson
> MF = Marisol Fuentes

MO   Mr Prior? How do you do.

JP   Pleased to meet you, Mr Ortega. Let me introduce our Purchasing Manager, Michelle Henderson.

MO   I'm glad to meet you, Ms Henderson.

MH   How do you do?

JP   Look, I'm sorry we're late, but we had a breakfast meeting.

MO   That's all right, Mr Prior. But I have a lunch appointment at twelve.

JP   Oh, I see. Right.

MO   Well, would you like a coffee before we start? Ms Henderson?

MH   I'd prefer orange juice if possible.

MO   Yes, of course. And Mr Prior?

JP   Yes, thank you. Black, please.

MO   Right, let's go to my office ... Marisol, could you send up two coffees and an orange juice, please?

MF   Certainly, Mr Ortega.

MO   Thank you. Well, did you have a good trip?

Exercises 4, 5 and 6

> JP = Jim Prior
> MO = Manuel Ortega
> MH = Michelle Henderson

JP   Well, as you know, we manufacture sailing boats. Produced nearly four hundred last year.

MO   Really? And is sailing popular in Miami?

JP   Oh, yes. Very.

MH   Do you sail, Mr Ortega?

MO   Not any more. But one of my daughters is a very good sailor. She's won competitions.

MH   That's great!

MO   Yes, we're very proud of her ... Anyway, back to Florida Marine.

MH   Right. Well, as Jim ... Mr Prior ... said, our production consists of sailing boats. But the problem is, there's not much room for expansion in the States.

MO   So that's why you're interested in Venezuela.

JP   Exactly.

MO   Well, South America's certainly an expanding market. We've been supplying resins here since 1985.

JP   Have you worked with other US companies, Mr Ortega?

MO   Yes. In fact last year we ...

UNIT 2 Part B

Exercise 1

Announcer:

> *Merci de votre compréhension.* Attention all passengers. Air France regrets to announce the late arrival of flight AF 171 from Hanoi and Bangkok. This is due to bad weather conditions over central Europe. The estimated time of arrival at Paris Charles de Gaulle Airport is now fifteen hundred hours, three pm local time. Thank you for your attention.

Exercises 3 and 4

> R = receptionist
> DBL = Dang Binh Luan

R   Can I help you, sir?

DBL   Good afternoon. I think the Vietnamese embassy has reserved rooms for us.

R   May I have your name, please?

DBL   Dang Binh Luan. Shall I spell it?

R   There's no need, sir ... Ah, yes. Two singles with bathroom for five nights.

DBL   That's it.

R   And how would you like to pay, sir?

DBL   By credit card.

R   Certainly.

R   Will you be having breakfast?

DBL   Yes, we will.

R   Well, it's served in the breakfast room between six and eleven.

DBL   OK.

R   And our restaurant's open for dinner every evening until ten.

DBL   Good.

R   Right, here are your room keys, sir. You're on the third floor – 314 and 316.

DBL   Thank you.

R   May we look after your luggage?

DBL   Yes, please.

R   Porter! Could you take these gentlemen's luggage to ...

UNIT 3 Part B

Exercises 1, 2 and 3

> AJ = Anna Jager
> JvD = Julia van Dijk

AJ   OK. I've noted down the information you need, Mrs van Dijk. But now I'd like to know what services Research Exchange offers.

JvD   Well, basically we take care of everything.

AJ   I don't believe you.

JvD   Well, almost everything anyway. As soon as I receive a list of the speakers from you, I'll send them a letter asking for an abstract of their talk for the conference programme.

84

AJ	Right …
JvD	Then, when you give me a full list of participants –
AJ	In March …
JvD	That's it Research Exchange will deal with their application forms and accommodation.
AJ	But who looks after the social programme?
JvD	We do. Once you approve the scientific programme, we'll work on the social programme together and I'll send out a full programme by July at the latest.
AJ	OK.
JvD	Then there's sponsorship from pharmaceutical companies. Jan Muller is our Sponsorship Manager, so he's responsible for that. But working directly with you, of course.
AJ	Of course Now what about transport to and from the hotels? Who –?
JvD	We do, Professor Jager.
AJ	"Professor Jager" – please call me Anna.
JvD	Pleasure. And I'm Julia.
AJ	Good … Right, Julia. Now, visa arrangements …

Exercises 4 and 5

CH = Centraal Hotel reservations
JC = Jennie Carpenter

CH	Centraal Hotel, good morning.
JC	Good morning. This is Jennie Carpenter of Research Exchange. I'm calling to ask about a group booking for rooms.
CH	Right … Research Exchange, you do medical conferences, don't you? We spoke together last year.
JC	That's it. Anyway, we've got another conference for next year. The 28th to the 31st of October.
CH	Just a minute, please … 28th to the 31st of October … Yes, that seems OK. How many rooms will you need?
JC	Well, at least a hundred.
CH	It's OK for the moment … When can you confirm?
JC	I'm not sure yet. Could I fix an appointment for Julia van Dijk to see your manager next week?
CH	OK. Hold on a moment and I'll check when he's free … either Thursday morning or Friday afternoon
JC	Shall we say Thursday morning at half past ten?
CH	That's the 13th.
JC	That's it. Thanks very much. Goodbye.
CH	Goodbye, Ms Carpenter, and thanks for calling.

Exercise 6

RH = Rembrandt Hotel reservations
JC = Jennie Carpenter

RH	Rembrandt Hotel, good morning.
JC	Good morning. My name's Jennie Carpenter of Research Exchange in Utrecht. We organise medical conferences.
RH	Hmm …?
JC	Do you do group bookings?
RH	Of course. But we're mainly a tourist hotel, you know, so we're full from May to –
JC	But it's for October next year.
RH	Oh. What dates exactly?
JC	The 28th to the 31st. And we'll need about a hundred rooms.

RH	Just a minute … No, we can't help you. We've got another conference that weekend, for two hundred people.
JC	Too bad. Thanks anyway. Goodbye.
RH	Bye.

UNIT 4 Part B

Exercises 1 and 2

IT = Ilona Tolnai
TM = Tom Masters

TM	… So if I understand your letter correctly, you're quite optimistic about the Internet's future here.
IT	Very optimistic, yes – especially for music sales. But I think it's a long-term investment.
TM	And you think the main customers will be young people?
IT	Oh, yes, I'm sure of that: especially in the beginning.
TM	But won't it be too expensive for them?
IT	At the moment, yes. But I'm sure prices will fall over the next two or three years.
TM	Yes, that's what usually happens … Oh, yes, and in your letter you said that most of the sales will be for popular music and jazz.
IT	Mm.
TM	But if we organised classical recordings with top orchestras, do you think they would sell on the Internet here?
IT	I'm not sure, Tom. In my opinion it's best to start with popular music.
TM	Hmm … well you're probably right … Now, what about website design?
IT	Well, in my view it must be as simple as possible with a totally secure ordering and payment system.
TM	Well that's for sure … And a last question, Ilona. Can Magyar Ventures help us on this?
IT	Yes, Tom. I believe we can.

Exercises 3 and 4

CJ = Charlie Jennings
TM = Tom Masters
NG = Nicci Garland

CJ	How was Budapest, Tom?
TM	Great. I think there's a future for us in central Europe.
CJ	Good. We'll talk about it later. Now the first thing is that new group, The Trainspotters. Did you listen to the cassette, Nicci?
NG	Yes, I did.
CJ	And what do you think?
NG	No good at all, Charlie.
TM	What d'you mean, no good? They're really exciting!
NG	No, Tom, I don't agree. They've got no style.
TM	But what about the singer? She's got talent, you must admit that.
NG	Well, she's not bad, I agree, but –
CJ	Look, we'll ask them to come to the studio for a test session, OK?
NG	If you want, Charlie. But I'm not optimistic.
TM	Right, I'll contact them this afternoon.
CJ	Good. And now on to Budapest Let's have your ideas, Tom.
TM	Well, it was a very useful trip. I think we …

UNIT 5 Part B
Exercises 1, 2 and 3

MH = Michelle Henderson
MO = Manuel Ortega

MH Right, we're here, in the administration block. Just behind us you can see the car park ...
MO Ah, yes.
MH ... and that building beside it is the staff restaurant.
MO Right.
MH Now, as you can see, there's one main entrance to Florida Marine, and then four roads. The first leads straight to the car park, and the second to the admin block and offices.
MO Uh huh ...
MH ... and that third road is the main entrance to the factory and leads directly into the delivery and storage area. And the last one here's the exit, out of the warehouse.
MO And what's that there, beside the main entrance?
MH Oh, that's the security building. The factory is guarded 24 hours a day.
MO Is security a problem?
MH Well, we have to be careful ... Anyway, let's look at the factory. You can see it's divided into four sections. First there's the delivery area, where we stock fibreglass resins. Next to the delivery area is the moulding area. That's where the hulls and decks are made. After that they're painted, here in the painting shop, and finally the finished boats are stored here, in the warehouse.
MO It looks very well organised.
MH Thank you. Now let's go and visit the factory and I'll show you around ...

Exercises 5 and 6

MH = Michelle Henderson
MO = Manuel Ortega

MH Well, basically there are three moulding processes – one for the hull, another for the deck and a third for the inside of the boat. First, a coat of special paint is put into the mould for the hull, and then it's covered with fibreglass resin.
MO And the next step is the deck.
MH No, the inside of the boat. Cabin walls, that sort of thing. Then we add the deck. And after that the boat's tested.
MO How do you mean, "tested"?
MH Well, it's put into water to check that it's waterproof. Then it goes to the warehouse.
MO Can I see this water test? It sounds interesting.
MH Sure. Come this way ...

UNIT 6 Part B
Exercises 1, 2 and 3

Sylvie Lavigne

... so I hope you'll agree that this project is a very good one, and will bring in a good return on investment.

I would like to remind you of my main points:
- There has been a steady growth of foreign investment in Vietnam since 1994.
- Inflation is under control and is not likely to rise.
- Commercial road transport will certainly increase.
- The country did not suffer from the Asian crisis a few years ago.
- And finally, because of our historical and cultural links, a French-sponsored bank syndicate has a good chance of doing business in Vietnam.

Right. Are there any questions?

Exercises 4 and 5

Q1 = Questioner 1
SL = Sylvie Lavigne
Q2 = Questioner 2

Q1 I can see that the number of buses fell slightly during the nineties. Was this because of competition from the railways?
SL No, I don't think so. But we must remember that Vietnam has 2,600 kilometres of rail track, so the government may want to use it more in the long term. But it needs to be modernised first.
Q2 The number of vans has trebled, hasn't it?
SL That's right.
Q2 Does the government expect this to continue?
SL Actually, I'm not sure. But we can be certain that lorry traffic will rise substantially over the next few years.
Q2 Thank you.

UNIT 7 Part B
Exercises 1 and 2

JC = Jennie Carpenter
IB = Ingrid Bendt

JC ... so you see, I'm afraid there are no more rooms at the Centraal Hotel.
IB Why is that?
JC Well, your application form was rather late, and most people want to stay in the centre of town.
IB I see. Well, what can we do?
JC I can still book you into the Park Hotel. It's very comfortable and there will be buses to the Conference Centre every day.
IB OK, you'd better do that then.
JC Right ... And there's another problem, I'm afraid.
IB Oh, no.
JC Yes. There are no suites left in the Park Hotel, only single rooms.
IB Professor Klein won't like that. He has to entertain visitors, you see. Aren't there any other hotels in the centre of town?
JC Well, there is the Excelsior, but it's very expensive.
IB So it's either a single room at the Park or a suite at the Excelsior?
JC That's the choice, I'm afraid.
IB Right. Look, could you reserve a suite at the Excelsior and I'll call you back tomorrow to confirm?

Exercises 3 and 4

IB = Ingrid Bendt
EB = Ellen Bakker

EB Research Exchange. May I help you?
IB Good morning. Could I speak to Ellen Bakker, please?
EB Speaking. Who's calling, please?
IB This is Ingrid Bendt, of Pharmasynthesis.
EB Oh yes, I sent you an e-mail an hour ago. Thanks for calling back so quickly.
IB That's OK ... Look, is the 31st of October the only time you can suggest?
EB I'm afraid so. You see, all the other presentation times are already reserved, and –
IB But it's the last day of the conference, and everybody will be so tired.
EB I know, Ms Bendt. But the problem is, we've only just received your application form. Other companies sent their forms in two or three months ago, so obviously they had priority.
IB Hmm ...
EB Look, I'll reserve you a place for the 31st of October, but if there's a cancellation for the other days, I'll contact you immediately.
IB Yes, OK. Thanks very much. Could you confirm that by e-mail, please?
EB Certainly. I'll send it today.
IB Thank you, Ms Bakker. Goodbye.
EB Goodbye.

UNIT 8 Part B

Exercises 1, 2, 3 and 4

R = Rico
TM = Tom Masters
NG = Nicci Garland

R Well, what do you think, Tom?
TM It sounds great.
R Nicci?
NG Very good.
R Glad you liked it.
TM OK, down to business. Have you all read the contract?
R Yeah ...
TM And?
R Well, we've got a few queries. (TM: Uh huh?) This clause 4. It specifies ten UK concerts a month from May to July. We reckon that's too many.
NG Well, how many do you suggest, Rico?
R What about eight a month? Two each weekend.
TM Yeah, that sounds OK ... Let's move on. Accommodation, clause 5. Any problems?
R The contract says double rooms, right?
TM That's it.
R Well, we don't agree. We want single rooms in good hotels.
TM Nicci?
NG You see, Rico, Macro Music isn't a rich company. So it's either double rooms in good hotels or single rooms in cheap hotels. Which do you want?
R OK, single rooms, I guess.
TM Right, let's look at money. Clause 6. We suggest a fixed amount per concert plus a percentage of ticket sales. What do you think?
R Well, it says here £240 per concert. That's not bad.

NG For the group, Rico. That's £60 per musician per concert ... Don't forget, you're not the Rolling Stones.
R Huh. And the percentage of ticket sales?
TM We'll calculate that at the end of the tour.
R OK, but I'll have to discuss it with the others.
TM Of course. Now on to clause 7 ...

Exercises 5 and 6

FB = Frankie Black
NG = Nicci Garland

FB Nicci?
NG That's me.
FB This is Frankie Black from *Music World*.
NG Hi, Frankie. How are you?
FB Fine ... Look, I'm calling about your new group –
NG The Trainspotters?
FB That's it. Well, I'd like to do an interview with Rico and their singer ...
NG That's Alex.
FB Alex, right.
NG Well, it's difficult at the moment because they're preparing a video and the UK tour starts next week.
FB Come on, Nicci, it'll be good publicity. All groups need publicity, that's how they sell their CDs.
NG Hmm.
FB Look, supposing I publish all their concert dates at the end of the interview. That way you get free advertising. It's good business, Nicci.
NG Yes, OK then. What about Saturday?
FB Saturday?
NG Why not?
FB You see, I usually play football on Saturday. Couldn't we make it Monday?
NG Sorry, Frankie. It's football or the interview. Saturday morning. Nine o'clock. Here at Macro Music.
FB OK, Nicci, I'll be there.
NG Good. Bye ...

UNIT 9 Part B

Exercises 1, 2 and 3

JR = Jack Ramsey
FC = Francisco Cordoves
JP = Jim Prior

JR I've never tasted Chilean wine before, Francisco. It's very good.
FC Yes, not bad, is it? It comes from the Valle Central, the centre of Chile.
JP Are you an expert on wine, Francisco?
FC Not really. I just enjoy it ...
JP So do I.
JP Well, Francisco, you know we're mainly interested in the Primaglass resin.
FC And not the other two?
JP Not in the short term. We'll only build twelve-metre boats to begin with.
FC I see.
JP But tomorrow we must be clear about what we want from Polycaracas.
JR The cheapest price for the best quality. That's what we always want!
FC Well, Polycaracas isn't necessarily the cheapest supplier, but they're reliable.

JP   Francisco's right, Jack. You've got to pay for good quality.

JR   Hmm. What do you think about possible discounts, Francisco?

FC   Well, it depends on how much we're going to buy ...

Exercises 4 and 5

MO = Manuel Ortega
JP = Jim Prior
JR = Jack Ramsey

Part 1

MO   Right, gentlemen. Let's start.

JP   Well, Mr Ortega, we're interested in doing business with Polycaracas. And today we're here to try to work out details.

MO   OK, but first I'd like to know when you plan to open in Venezuela and what you'll manufacture here ... you know, the general picture.

JP   Right. Jack, can you fill Mr Ortega in on that?

JR   Sure. Well, we hope to start production in about six months. At first we'll only build twelve-metre boats as ...

Part 2

MO   Thank you, Mr Ramsey. That was very clear. So, if I understand you correctly, you're interested in buying our Primaglass resin in fixed quantities per month over the first year.

JP   No, not quite.

MO   Oh?

JP   Not fixed quantities, Mr Ortega. Probably about two thousand kilograms a month for the first three months rising to five or six thousand by the end of the year.

MO   I see. That's no problem.

JP   Good. Now, about delivery times.

MO   If the resin's in stock, three days after the order.

JR   And if not?

MO   Well, that depends ... You see, if you give us a fixed quantity every month, I can guarantee it will be in stock.

JP   Right, I'll think about it. Let's move on to prices, shall we?

MO   Yes, Mr Prior – the difficult part.

UNIT 10   Part B
Exercises 1 and 2

LVN = Le Van Nam
GL = Gerhard Leinhof
O = Others

LVN   We hope your helicopter trip didn't spoil your lunch ...?

O   No ... Not at all ...

LVN   That's good ... Well, this morning we flew over the Hanoi end of the motorway site and we saw the traffic jams. These are mainly caused by the hundreds of lorries that leave Hanoi every day. Now, a motorway would solve that problem and also improve communications between Haiphong and the northern provinces because of the modernised connecting road.

GL   Excuse me, Mr Le.

LVN   Yes, Dr Leinhof?

GL   Is there a lot of traffic from the northern provinces to Haiphong?

LVN   Yes, there is, and it's going to increase. But at the moment the maximum possible speed is often only 30 kilometres an hour, because of the roads.

GL   Thank you. Oh, and another thing ...

LVN   Yes?

GL   Do you know the average delay of each lorry?

LVN   It's difficult to calculate, Dr Leinhof, but probably about two hours. And I'm sure this has a negative effect on business in the region.

Exercises 4, 5 and 6

NMT = Nguyen Minh Tuan
MR = Martin Reynolds

NMT   Well, Mr Reynolds. Have you enjoyed your visit?

MR   Yes, it's been very interesting.

NMT   And the helicopter flight yesterday?

MR   Well, frankly, Mr Nguyen, I don't like flying very much ...

NMT   Neither do I.

MR   ... but it was very useful.

NMT   Yes, it's necessary to see everything.

MR   ... Mmm, this is delicious. What's it called, Mr Nguyen?

NMT   *Bun cha*. It's a speciality of north Vietnam.

MR   And what is it made from?

NMT   Green vegetables, noodles and herbs, and the meat is pork. It's grilled then served in a special sauce.

MR   Well, I've eaten in lots of Vietnamese restaurants in Paris, but the food was never as good as this.

NMT   You have to visit a country to really taste its cuisine, Mr Reynolds. But some of the Vietnamese restaurants in Paris aren't bad.

MR   Do you often visit Paris?

NMT   Two or three times a year normally. We do a lot of trade with France, you know.

MR   Yes, of course. Well, the next time you come, you must let me invite you to a Vietnamese dinner.

NMT   Thank you. It would be a pleasure.

MR   But on one condition – you choose the restaurant!

UNIT 11   Part B
Exercises 1 and 2

M1 = first man
WL = Wim Lubbers

M1   Excuse me, about the drinks party this evening. How long will it last?

WL   Oh, about an hour, I should think.

M1   OK. Oh, and another thing. Is it formal? You know, evening dress?

WL   No, not at all. There will just be a short welcome speech, then drinks.

M1   I see. Fine, thank you.

WL   You're welcome.

Exercises 3 and 4

M2 = second man
WL = Wim Lubbers

M2   I have a question, Mr Lubbers ...

WL   Yes?

M2   ... about the trip to the Rijksmuseum. Well, the thing is, my wife's English is not very good. Do you know if the guide speaks French?

WL   I'm not sure ... Look, I'll ask the Rijksmuseum if they can provide a French-speaking guide.

M2   Thank you very much.

Exercises 5 and 6

W1 = first woman
WL = Wim Lubbers

W1 Mr Lubbers. My husband's just come back from the boat trip on the canals.
WL Did he enjoy it?
W1 No, not much. It was raining.
WL Oh, what a pity.
W1 But that's not the problem, Mr Lubbers. Look, on the programme it says that lunch is included, right?
WL Ye-es …
W1 But he had to pay over 15 euros for a half-bottle of wine. And it wasn't very good.
WL I'm sorry about that. But you see, wine wasn't included in the price …

Exercises 7 and 8

W2 = second woman
WL = Wim Lubbers

W2 Mr Lubbers?
WL Yes?
W2 Could you tell me if there are vegetarian menus for the banquet tomorrow evening?
WL Did you ask for one on your application form?
W2 I'm afraid not. I forgot.
WL Don't worry. I'll look after it.
W2 Thanks so much.

UNIT 12 Part B
Exercises 1 and 2

TM = Tom Masters
IT = Ilona Tolnai

Part 1
TM Ilona? It's Tom.
IT Hi, Tom. How are things?
TM Well, all right … but the saxophone player's gone sick.
IT Is it serious?
TM The doctors think it is. He'll have to go into hospital.
IT Oh, no!
TM And I've got to find a replacement by tomorrow …

Part 2
TM And how are things at your end?
IT Everything's ready – most of the tickets are sold, and –
TM What about the hotel? Where is it?
IT In the centre of Budapest, but I'm not sure which one. Marianna's looking after that.
TM You haven't checked it yourself?
IT Tom, Marianna's perfectly capable of booking a hotel!
TM Well, yes, I'm sure, but …

Part 3
TM Now, about the rest of the tour …
IT Yes?
TM Don't you think we should hire a professional interpreter? I mean Marianna's quite young, and …
IT Look, Tom. She speaks four languages and she's had a lot of experience with Magyar Ventures. I'm sure she'll deal with the interpreting very well. And anyway, do you know how much professional interpreters cost?
TM Yes, there is that …

Part 4
IT Oh, by the way, Tom. We haven't received those CDs you promised. A thousand, wasn't it?
TM What?!
IT And we need them by Thursday at the latest.
TM Look, I'll get onto this straight away and call you right back.

Exercises 3 and 4

TM = Tom Masters
IT = Ilona Tolnai
BP = Bill Palmer

TM Well, how's the tour going?
IT Very well. Marianna called me from Poland last night. Everything's fine.
TM And what about that new saxophone player?
IT Marianna says he's very talented.
TM Good.
IT Right, let's start … We're going to look at two things this afternoon. First, on-line CD sales in Hungary, and then the possibilities of direct downloading of music from our website. Let's take CD sales first. This slide shows the various stages … To begin with, we must form a team to process telephone orders and deal with enquiries.
BP And complaints.
IT Yes, Bill. And complaints … I suggest a small team headed by an English-speaking person who can liaise with Macro Music if necessary.
TM I agree. Now what about storage?
IT We already have a very efficient warehouse thirty kilometres from Budapest, but it'll need some reorganisation. I'll look after that.
TM OK.
IT Now on to payment. Our Accounts Department can deal with that. No problem.
TM Are you sure, Ilona? Won't you need a separate team to cover this?
IT No, I don't think so. Certainly not in the early stages.
TM Hmm. And what about transport?
IT Well, we usually work with a courier company that's very good.

Answer key

Before you start

1
1 C   2 D   3 A   4 E
5 B

A Reading and writing

1
1 Managing Director
2 Juanita Castro
3 Carla Naranjo
4 assistant
5 Marisol Fuentes

3
1 c   2 b   3 a   4 b
5 a

4 *Model answer*
Dear Mr Prior,
Thank you for your letter of April 5.
We are very interested in your plans
to open a production site here and
would be very pleased to meet you
in Venezuela in June.
I would like to suggest Tuesday
June 5 at 10 am. Please confirm this.
I look forward to seeing you on
June 5.
Yours sincerely
Manuel Ortega

B Listening

1
1 c   2 b   3 a

2
1 c   2 b   3 c

3
1 How do
2 Pleased to
3 Let ... introduce
4 glad to meet
5 would ... like

4
1 True
2 False (not any more)
3 False (there's not much room for
   expansion in the States)
4 True
5 False (they've worked with other
   US companies)

5
1 They made nearly 400 last year.
2 She is a very good sailor; she's
   won competitions.

3 Because South America is an
   expanding market.
4 Polycaracas have been supplying
   resins in South America since
   1985.

6
1 manufacture
2 Produced
3 production consists of
4 expansion
5 expanding market
6 supplying
7 worked with

C Speaking

1
1 C   2 D   3 E   4 A
5 B

2 *Model answers*
1 Fine, thanks. How about you?
2 Pleased to meet you.
3 Yes, fine, thanks.
4 Yes, I am. Nice to meet you.
5 How do you do.
6 Yes, it was at the conference in
   Krakow.

3
1 run
2 involves
3 reports to
4 consists of
5 takes part in

Before you start

1
1 D   2 A   3 E   4 F
5 C   6 B

A Reading and writing

1
1 True
2 False (road transport is
   inefficient/road communications
   are inadequate)
3 True
4 False (it will need around
   $75 million)
5 False (25% of the sum will come
   from local sources, so this cannot
   be correct)
6 True

2 *Model answer*
Dear Martin
Many thanks for your kind offer. My
colleague and I will arrive on Air
France flight AF 171 which will land
at Charles de Gaulle Airport at 13.30
on 14 June (your time). We are
staying at the Hotel de la Tour. Just
to confirm our appointment – it's on
15 June at 9 o'clock.
It'll be good to see you again!
Best wishes
Luan

B Listening

1
1 b   2 a   3 b

2
1 see
3 How
4 This
5 do
6 Pleased

3
1 c   2 a   3 b   4 c
5 a   6 c

4
1 I help you
2 I have your name
3 how would you like to
4 you be having
5 we look after your

C Speaking

1 *Model answers*
1 Where do I leave from, please?/
   Where does the flight leave from?
2 What time must I check in?/
   What time is check-in?
3 Why is the flight late?/
   Why is there a delay?
4 Can I smoke on the plane?
5 When do we get to London?/
   When does the flight arrive in
   London?

2
Speaker A
1 Arrival time: 17.15
2 Flight number: BA 7083
3 Cost of ticket: 745 euros
4 Flight delay: 45 minutes
5 Check-in time: 4 o'clock

Speaker B
1 Take-off time: 14.30
2 Cost of ticket: 475 euros
3 Original arrival time of flight:
  18.15
4 Flight number: SW 8174
5 Check-in time: 5.30

UNIT 3

Before you start

1
1 B 2 A 3 B 4 A
5 B 6 A

A Reading and writing

1
1 Jennie Carpenter
2 Julia van Dijk
3 Jan Muller
4 Ellen Bakker
5 Wim Lubbers

2
1 True
2 False (this is their first contact)
3 True
4 False (Fischer organised one last
  year)
5 False (van Dijk must contact
  Jager's secretary)

3 *Model answer*
Dear Julia,
It was good to meet you yesterday. I
am just writing to confirm what we
discussed.
I agreed to provide you with a list of
speakers by February at the latest.
I also agreed to prepare a list of
conference participants by the end of
March. In early April I will finalise
the scientific programme.
In the meantime, I hope to hear
from you soon to confirm the date of
our visit to the Utrecht Conference
Centre.
I look forward to visiting the
Conference Centre.
Regards
Anna Jager

B Listening

1
the social programme – 4
a list of speakers – 1
transport – 6
a list of participants – 2
application forms and
accommodation – 3
visa arrangements – 7
sponsorship – 5

2
1 I'd like to know
2 take care of
3 As soon as ... I'll send
4 deal with
5 looks after
6 Once ... we'll work ... I'll send
7 responsible for
8 what about

3
AJ
provide list of speakers
provide list of participants
approve scientific programme
RE
send letter to speakers
organise accommodation
send out full programme
organise transport
both
work on social programme
work on sponsorship

4
1 True
2 False (she is only making an
  enquiry)
3 False (next week)
4 False (van Dijk will visit the
  hotel)

5
1 a 2 b 3 c

6
1 c 2 b 3 c

C Speaking

1 *Model answers*
1 Hello, my name's ...
2 Can I speak to ...
3 Hold on a minute, please.
4 Who's calling, please?
5 Putting you through.
6 Can you repeat that, please?
7 I'm afraid he/she's out at the
  moment.
8 Can I leave a message?

2
1 e 2 f 3 b 4 g
5 c 6 a 7 d

UNIT 4

Before you start

1
1 begin
2 agree
3 think
4 say
5 view
6 disagree

A Reading and writing

1
1 False (only a project at present)
2 True
3 True
4 True
5 False (he writes "if we decide to
  go ahead with this ...")
6 True

2 *Model answers*
1 we are very interested in the
  possibilities of the Internet
2 what do you think about the
  future of the Internet ...?
3 will the downloading of music ...
  become popular?
4 Which kinds of music will be
  downloaded?

3 *Model answer*
Dear Mr Masters
Many thanks for your letter of
4 September.
In my opinion, this is a very
interesting project which could be
profitable in the long term. As you
know, the Internet is developing
quickly in Europe, and the
downloading of music is already
very popular, especially with young
people.
Concerning the kind of music to be
downloaded, I think it should be
about 80% popular and jazz music
and 20% classical.
I would be very interested to meet
you to discuss the possibility of
future co-operation between our two
companies.
Yours sincerely
Ilona Tolnai

B Listening

1
1 optimistic
2 short term
3 at first
4 expensive
5 drop
6 popular
7 classical
8 secure
9 interested
10 yes

2
1 think
2 I'm sure of that
3 won't it
4 I'm sure
5 do you think
6 In my opinion
7 probably right

8 in my view
9 for sure
10 believe

3
1 True
2 False (she says "No good at all")
3 False (he says "they're really
  exciting")
4 True
5 True

4
1 No good at all
2 really exciting
3 got no style
4 must admit
5 we'll ask

C Speaking

1
1 D   2 A   3 E   4 C
5 B

2
1 c   2 e   3 a   4 h
5 f   6 b   7 g   8 d

UNIT 5

Before you start

1
1 We do not accept responsibility
  for losses
2 Switch off printer/printer off after
  use
3 Do not park your car here
4 You are requested not to take
  photographs
5 Personnel must arrive before ten
  o'clock
6 Staff must not make personal calls
7 No entry without authorisation

A Reading and writing

1
1 True
2 False (trip planned for following
  month)
3 True
4 False (wants to go the "last week
  in September")
5 False (wants to see either
  Henderson or Prior)

2 *Model answer*
Dear Mr Ortega
Thank you for your fax of August 8.
Although Jim Prior is on vacation in
September, I will be pleased to show
you round our factory. May I suggest
September 27 at 9 o'clock? After the
visit, I would be pleased to invite you
to lunch.

Along with this fax, I am sending
you a map with directions of how to
get from the centre of Miami to
Florida Marine.
I look forward to seeing you.
Sincerely yours
Michelle Henderson

3
1 take
2 turn
3 Go/Continue
4 take
5 Go/Continue

B Listening

1
Administration block D
Security building A
Delivery and storage area E
Warehouse H
Staff restaurant C
Moulding area F
Car park B
Painting shop G

2
1 fibreglass resins are stocked
2 hulls and decks are made
3 boats are painted
4 finished boats are stored

3
1 leads
2 is guarded
3 it's divided
4 are made
5 are/'re painted
6 are stored

4
1 F   2 B   3 E   4 A
5 C

5 (in any order)
1 hull
2 inside
3 deck

6
1 c   2 b   3 c

C Speaking

1
1 like
2 What
3 Could
4 When
5 call
6 Where

2
1 c   2 e   3 d   4 a
5 f   6 g   7 h   8 b

Before you start

1
1 a   2 b   3 b

A Reading and writing

1
1 b   2 a   3 a   4 c
5 b   6 a   7 c   8 b

2
1 b   2 c   3 b   4 a
5 a   6 b

3 *Model answer*
Inflation
This fell from 37.5% in 1992 to
16.9% in 1995. It continued to
decrease, and was down to 7% in
1999.

Exports
These rose steadily in the 1990s.
They grew from $2.4 billion in 1992
to $5.3 billion in 1995. This figure
had almost doubled to reach $9.8
billion in 1999.

Lorries
The number of lorries in Vietnam
rose by about 10% in the 1990s –
from around 95,000 in 1992 to
nearly 105,000 in 1999.

B Listening

1
1 a   2 b

2
1 c   2 b   3 b   4 c
5 a

3
1 steady growth
2 likely
3 will certainly
4 a good chance

4
1 True
2 False (it has 2,600)
3 False (they need to be
  modernised)
4 True
5 False (lorry traffic will rise)

5
1 fell slightly
2 may want
3 trebled
4 certain ... rise substantially

6
1 fell slightly
2 certain
3 rise substantially
4 may want
5 trebled

C Speaking

1

Model answer – Japanese investment in Vietnam

Japanese investment in Vietnam nearly trebled between 1992 and 1998. It rose slightly from $1,340 million in 1992 to $1,450 million the following year. Then it increased threefold, to reach $3,495 million by 1998.

Model answer – Vietnam's industrial growth

Between 1991 and 1998, industrial growth in Vietnam rose a little, then fell. It stood at 10.4% in 1991, went up to 14.5% in 1995 then dropped by over two points to 12.1% in 1998. However, it is expected to begin to rise again in the early years of the 21st century.

UNIT 7

Before you start

1
B

A Reading and writing

1
1 True
2 False (worked with a part-time secretary)
3 True
4 True
5 False (three conferences outside the Netherlands)
6 True

2
1 performed
2 runs/ran
3 founded
4 consists of
5 expand

3

The following should be noted:
1 "stand" box should be ticked
2 Title should be completed: "Beyond beta-blockers"
Preferred times should be circled: 29/10 morning and 30/10 afternoon
Other equipment: video cassette player
3 Klein, Johannes (Prof)
Foucault, Marie-Laure (Dr)
Bendt, Ingrid (Ms)
Centraal Hotel should be underlined
single room(s): 2; suite(s): 1

B Listening

1
1 a   2 b   3 c   4 b
5 c

2
1 application form sent in late
2 comfortable/buses to Conference Centre
3 no suites left at Park Hotel
4 because Professor Klein has to entertain visitors
5 either ... or
6 reserve a suite at the Excelsior; she will confirm tomorrow

3
1 all the conference participants will be tired
2 other times already reserved by companies who sent in their forms earlier
3 she will reserve 31/10, but contact Ingrid Bendt if there's a cancellation for the other days

4
1 You see
2 But the problem is
3 so obviously
4 Look ... if there's ... I'll
5 Certainly

5 *Model answer*
To: Ingrid Bendt
From: Ellen Bakker
Confirming our telephone conversation today. I have reserved your presentation for 31 October. But if there are cancellations for either of the other days, I will contact you immediately.
Regards
Ellen Bakker

C Speaking

1
1 relocate
2 employ
3 sell
4 buy
5 start
6 change job
7 raise
8 leave

2
1 c   2 f   3 i   4 a
5 b   6 h   7 j   8 g
9 d   10 e

UNIT 8

Before you start

1
1 open

2 don't ... begin
3 don't ... record
4 advertise
5 ask

A Reading and writing

1
1 a   2 c   3 c   4 a

2
1 What we suggest is a copyrighted performance ...
2 ... we could sell a very attractive collection ...
3 ... we could record parts of operas ...

3 *Model answer*
Dear Mr Masters
Thank you for your letter of 29 October. I have discussed your suggestions with the conductor and some of the musicians, and these are our reactions.
We agree that copyrighted performances for the Internet are an interesting idea, and suggest that these should be combined with CD sales. However, we are not enthusiastic about the idea of songs and waltzes, which is not very original. Our suggestion is for a copyrighted performance of well-known film music or alternatively, selections from Duke Ellington. We are sure that these would be more interesting for young people.
I look forward to hearing your response to my suggestions.
Best wishes
Gustav Richter

B Listening

1
1 number of concerts
2 accommodation
3 money

2
1 B   2 C   3 A

3
1 a
2 eight concerts a month
3 b
4 single rooms in cheap hotels
5 c
6 £60 ... concert

4
1 do you suggest
2 What about
3 You see
4 So ... either ... or
5 We suggest
6 Don't forget

5

1 True
2 False (he wants to interview Rico and Alex)
3 False (they're preparing a video)
4 False (he wants to do an interview)
5 True
6 False (agrees to an interview on Saturday)

6

1 ... because they're preparing a video and the UK tour starts next week.
2 ... that's how they sell their CDs.
3 ... supposing I publish all their concert dates at the end of the interview.
4 That way you get free advertising.
5 What about Saturday?
6 You see, I usually play football on Saturday.
7 Couldn't we make it Monday?

C Speaking

1

1 I suggest starting with/that we start with ...
2 In order to ...
3 We could ask for ...
4 because of ...
5 Why don't we organise ...

2

1 in order to
2 so
3 because
4 That way
5 because of

UNIT 9

Before you start

1

1 C 2 D 3 A 4 E
5 B

A Reading and writing

1

1 year
2 factory
3 hired
4 manager
5 equipment
6 staff
7 supplier
8 contract

2

1 False (factory to open the following spring)
2 False ("near" Caracas)

3 True
4 False (Francisco Cordoves's job)
5 True
6 False (contract not yet negotiated)

3

Venelite 100 kg – 170 dollars; small boats and canoes
Primaglass 250 kg – 460 dollars
Venemix 100 kg – 220 dollars; motor boats

4 *Model answer*

... Let me have your comments, please.
– What discount can we get on Venelite?
– Could we use Primaglass for canoes?
– Do you think Mr Ortega would accept payment 90 days after delivery, and what about the possibilities of getting a reduction on Venemix (after all, it's very expensive).
– Can we get him to guarantee a minimum delivery time?
– Finally, do you think he'll agree to a one-year contract, or will he want longer? Please reply ASAP.
Yours, Jim

B Listening

1

wine
supplier
Chile
discounts
quality
tomorrow

2 *Model answers*

1 It is very good.
2 It comes from the Valle Central in Chile.
3 He wants the cheapest price for the best quality.
4 They are not the cheapest supplier, but they are reliable.
5 You've got to pay for good quality.

3

1 mainly interested in
2 short term
3 cheapest price ... best
4 cheapest ... reliable
5 possible discounts

4

1 b 2 a 3 b 4 b
5 a

5

1 b 2 b 3 a 4 c

6

1 fixed

2 rise
3 first
4 days
5 stock
6 orders
7 guarantee

C Speaking

1

1 of 2 in 3 by 4 to
5 on

2

1 G 2 H 3 E 4 A
5 B 6 D 7 F 8 C

UNIT 10

Before you start

1

1 It is 50 kilometres long.
2 It is 10.5 metres wide.
3 The road surface is five centimetres thick.

A Reading and writing

1

1 b 2 c 3 b 4 a

2 B

3 *Model answer*

... We are very pleased to accept. We are looking forward to our visit to Vietnam, and hope that it will lead to a fruitful co-operation.
Yours sincerely
Martin Reynolds

B Listening

1

1 True
2 False (motorway would improve communications)
3 True
4 False (probably about two hours' delay)
5 True

2

1 the hundreds
2 30 kilometres
3 about two

3

1 C 2 D 3 A 4 E
5 B

4

flying
trips to France
Vietnamese restaurants in Paris
Vietnamese specialities

5

1 b 2 c 3 a 4 b
5 a

6 that Nguyen Minh Tuan chooses the restaurant

6
1 Have you enjoyed
2 been very interesting
3 delicious ... called
4 never as good
5 let me invite
6 would be a

C Speaking

1
Answers may vary, but in most English-speaking countries the following apply:
1 N   2 A   3 N   4 N
5 A   6 N   7 A   8 N
9 A   10 N

2
1 C   2 F   3 A   4 D
5 E   6 B

UNIT 11

Before you start

1
Can you tell me when the drinks party starts?
And where will it be?
How long will it last, please?
And will there be any food?
Thank you.

A Reading and writing

1
1 Amsterdam State University
2 plenary lecture
3 poster exhibition
4 Dr Isabelle Carrier
5 Dr Margaret Boka
6 Zimbabwe
7 one hour
8 15.30
9 drinks party
10 20.00

2
1 In the auditorium
2 28 October
3 10.30
4 12.30–14.00
5 12.00
6 In room 107
7 Dr Boka's and Dr Nabokova's
8 18.30

3 *Errors:*
Dear Ms Bakker
I <u>didn't receive</u> a conference programme yet. You <u>said</u> me on the telephone last week that my presentation would be on 28 October <u>at</u> the afternoon. <u>Thank you to tell</u> <u>me</u> the exact <u>hour</u>.
Also, <u>you must to confirm me</u> that a video player will be available. And <u>final</u>, I <u>want</u> a list of all the other conference participants.
<u>I am thanking you</u> for your help.
Yours <u>faithfully</u>
Marie-Laure Foucault

Corrected version:
Dear Ms Bakker
I haven't yet received a conference programme*. You told me on the telephone last week that my presentation would be on 28 October in the afternoon. Please could you tell me the exact time.
Also, please confirm that a video player will be available. And finally, I would like a list of all the other conference participants.
Thank you for your help.
Yours sincerely
Marie-Laure Foucault

*I haven't received a conference programme yet is also possible

4 *Model answer*
Dear Dr Foucault
Thank you for your e-mail.
Your presentation is on 28 October from 17.00 to 17.30. I have reserved a video player for you.
I am surprised you haven't yet received a conference programme, and have sent another in the post today.
A complete list of participants will be sent to you after the conference.
Please let me know if you have any further queries.
Regards
Ellen Bakker

B Listening

1
1 b   2 c

2
1 Excuse me ... will it last
2 another thing ... You know ...

3
1 False (his wife wants to visit the museum)
2 False (obviously false, he's speaking English now)
3 True
4 False (his wife needs a French-speaking guide)
5 True

4
1 have a question
2 the thing is
3 you know if

5
1 c   2 a

6
1 a pity.
2 not the problem
3 right?
4 sorry about that.

7
1 b   2 c

8
1 you tell me
2 you ask for
3 afraid not.
4 worry. ... look after it.

C Speaking

1
1 JC   2 WL   3 WL
4 EB   5 EB   6 JC

2
a 3   b 5   c 6   d 1
e 2   f 4

3
1 when Dr Carrier's presentation is, please
2 It's at 11.30 in room 103
3 how long it will last
4 half an hour
5 what time is lunch

UNIT 12

Before you start

1
1 in charge
2 reports
3 down
4 look
5 responsible

A Reading and writing

1
1 Working with them is very exciting
2 Websites, distribution of computer equipment and the concert business
3 In central Europe
4 (Apart from Internet activities) advertising, ticket sales, travel and accommodation
5 No
6 By sending Bill Palmer to Budapest
7 Next month
8 They're great/They're going to be a big success

2
1 to look after
2 at the latest

3 deal with
4 report
5 By
6 in charge
7 responsible

B Listening

1
1 b   2 c   3 a   4 c

2
1 He is ill
2 Find a replacement
3 Yes
4 look after
5 Hire a professional interpreter
6 deal with
7 c
8 They haven't arrived in Budapest
9 at the latest

3
1 False (it will be about on-line CD sales and direct downloading)
2 False (she wants an English-speaking person to head the team)
3 True
4 False (the Accounts Department can deal with payment)
5 False (Magyar Ventures works with a good courier company)

4
1 form ... team
2 headed by
3 need ... reorganisation. ... look after
4 to cover this

C Speaking

1
1 reports to
2 supervises
3 manages
4 deals with
5 responsibility

2
1 D   2 H   3 E   4 B
5 G   6 A   7 C   8 F

DELTA Publishing
39 Alexandra Road
Addlestone
Surrey KT15 2PQ
United Kingdom

Text © David Kerridge 2000
Design and illustration © Delta Publishing 2000

First published 2000
International edition ISBN 1 900783 40 1

Design and illustration by Oxford Designers & Illustrators
Printed in Malta by Progress Press Co. Ltd

Photograph acknowledgements
The author and publishers wish to acknowledge, with thanks, the following photographic sources:

Art Directors and TRIP Photograph Library pp 8 (photograph Color Stock); 16 (photograph C Ryan); 18 (photograph E Knight); 24 (photograph T Bognar); 36 (photograph Viesti Associates); 38 (photograph Ask Images); 42 (photograph Colin Baker); 56 (photograph M Barlow); 62 (photograph T Bognar); 66 (photograph Eric Smith)

Camera Press pp 10 (photograph Fred Adler); 20 (photograph Gratton/Vision/Grazia Neri)

Redferns pp 50 (photograph Nicky J Sims); 54 (photograph Odile Noel); 72 (photograph Mick Hutson)

Topham Picturepoint pp 6; 14

Cover photo: Image Bank

With acknowledgement to Eric Kerridge (Rico) for the guitar extract in Unit 8.

The publishers have made every effort to trace the copyright holders but if they have inadvertently overlooked any, they will be pleased to make the necessary acknowledgements at the first opportunity.